DIGITAL MINDS

12 Things Every Business Needs to Know About Digital Marketing

D0054893

Produced by:

FriesenPress
Suite 300 – 852 Fort Street
Victoria, BC, Canada V8W 1H8

www.friesenpress.com

Distributed to the trade by The Ingram Book Company

CONTENTS

ACKNOWLEDGMENTS

WSI would like to acknowledge the Consultants who contributed to this book. Without their valuable time and expertise, this book would not have been possible. We'd also like to recognize all Corporate Team members who helped put the book together.

INTRODUCTION:
THE DIGITAL WORLD

Technology and the Internet are in flux. Some of the most popular companies in the world – Apple, Google, Facebook, Microsoft and Samsung – are from the tech and Internet industries. The platforms, devices and operating systems being developed by these tech giants are changing the way we interact with the Internet and each other.

As the Internet continues to shift the way we seek information, technology is working equally as hard to change the way we consume that information. But change is difficult; people don't like to adapt, whether to a new house or a different smartphone. As hard as it is for people to face change, we now live in a digital world. And in this new world, traditional forms of advertising don't work as well as they used to.

We still watch TV and listen to the radio, sure, but the ads we see and hear on these mediums are untargeted and reach us outside of the buying cycle. People now search for information before, or even during, the purchasing process. The notion of a person watching TV and running out to buy something they see in a commercial is no longer reality. Now, the buying cycle consists of a customer in a store searching their mobile device for information about a product they're holding in their hands. Enter digital marketing, something else new and scary. First businesses dismissed the Internet as a fad, claiming they didn't need a website. Now that those businesses are online, they're told to use social media, do mobile marketing and pay Google when people click on their ads and visit their website. With so many ever-changing options, digital marketing can be confusing. And indeed, many businesses have chosen to bury their heads in the sand instead of accepting the challenge of digital marketing. But savvy business managers and entrepreneurs who saw the immense opportunity of the digital landscape have certainly reaped the benefits. Luckily for you and your business, digital marketing is in its infancy and there's still plenty of time to catch up to speed.

So where does digital marketing and technology fit in today's online world? The short answer is everywhere. The more ways a business can enhance their online presence, the better. And as each new digital trend emerges, the businesses that are best at adapting and making it work for them are winning online.

This book is divided into 12 chapters, each one written by either a WSI Consultant or a member of the Corporate Team who has specific expertise on their topic. The book can be read cover-to-cover or digested one chapter at a time (in any order). It was written as a guide to digital marketing for business managers and entrepreneurs who have yet to take the plunge and don't know where to start.

It's the hope of the WSI team and all authors that this work will help you and your company dive into digital marketing and never look back.

1

THE DIGITAL LANDSCAPE:

FRAMEWORK AND STRATEGY

By Husam Jandal

Business owners and entrepreneurs are starting to recognize the importance and value of an online presence.
And while a universal acceptance of digital marketing is a
huge step forward for the marketing industry, many business owners are in such a rush to get online that they fail
to develop a proper strategy for the move into the digital
space. Going digital for the sake of having a website and
using social media is not the answer; by themselves and in
the wrong hands, these things are often misused or incor-
rectly implemented. The real key to generating a great
return on investment (ROI) with Internet marketing is
using your business goals to develop a dedicated strategy.

Meet the Digital Royal Family

There are four main pillars of digital marketing emerging as the 'Digital Royal Family' – cornerstones upon which to build successful digital marketing campaigns. These are the areas every entrepreneur and business manager needs to know and understand in order to be successful in the digital age of the Internet.

Content is Still King

While the phrase 'Content is King' has become an over-used cliché, the statement is as true as ever. King Content is the lifeblood of digital marketing. Without content, the strategies and techniques discussed in this book wouldn't be effective.

So what exactly is content? In the context of the Internet, content is anything digital: website copy, blog posts, infographics, newsletters, whitepapers, campaigns, videos, and web and mobile applications. Anything designed to bring value to the audience consuming it – whether in the form of entertainment or information – is considered content.

The Internet is saturated with mediocre content, which places an even greater importance on creating content with a clearly defined strategy based on specific goals and expectations. Figure 1 outlines the drastic degree to which defined content strategies are being implemented or planned by both brand marketers and agency clients, which further indicates that content is King of the Digital Royal Family and Ruler of the Internet Realm.

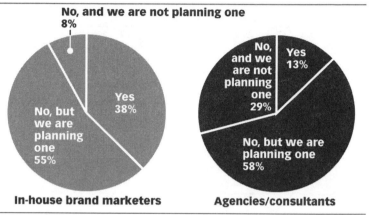

Brand Marketers and Agency Clients Worldwide that Have a Defined Content Marketing Strategy, Aug 2012
% of total

No, and we are not planning one
8%

Yes
38%

No, but we are planning one
55%

In-house brand marketers

No, and we are not planning one
29%

Yes
13%

No, but we are planning one
58%

Agencies/consultants

Note: n=654 in-house marketers working for a brand; n=513 agencies/consultants; numbers may not add up to 100% due to rounding; read as 38% of in-house marketers working for a brand say their company has a defined content marketing strategy while 13% of agencies/consultants said their clients had a defined content marketing strategy

Source: Outbrain and Econsultancy, "Content Marketing Survey Report 2012," Oct 3, 2012

146179   www.**eMarketer**.com

Figure 1: Content Marketing Strategy

Digital Advertising is Queen

Next in the hierarchy of digital marketing is Queen Digital Advertising. Stats show that digital ad spending has steadily increased 15% year over year and is projected to continue at this pace into 2016 (see Figure 2). Regardless of geographical region, the stats say the same thing: digital advertising spend is on the rise. Businesses can't afford to ignore the shift to digital advertising any longer or they risk getting left behind the competition.

Digital Ad Spending Growth Worldwide, by Region, 2010-2016
% change

	2010	2011	2012	2013	2014	2015	2016
Middle East & Africa	70.0%	55.8%	47.9%	47.4%	38.5%	30.0%	26.5%
Latin America	27.0%	34.0%	37.0%	23.0%	28.0%	18.0%	16.0%
Asia-Pacific	20.0%	23.1%	25.0%	19.0%	16.0%	14.0%	13.0%
Eastern Europe	32.7%	38.4%	18.9%	17.3%	15.5%	13.0%	9.0%
North America	15.6%	21.5%	16.6%	13.8%	12.4%	9.0%	6.8%
Western Europe	15.5%	13.9%	10.6%	11.0%	10.0%	7.4%	6.6%
Worldwide	**17.5%**	**20.6%**	**17.8%**	**15.1%**	**13.7%**	**10.8%**	**9.3%**

Note: includes advertising that appears on desktop and laptop computers as well as mobile phones and tablets, and includes all the various formats of advertising on those platforms; excludes SMS, MMS and P2P messaging-based advertising
Source: eMarketer, Dec 2012

148094   www.e**Marketer**.com

Figure 2: Digital Ad Spending Growth, Worldwide, by Region

Mobile is Prince

Things get a little crazy starting with the children of the Digital Royal Family. They're young, wild at heart and slightly unpredictable, but their potential is limitless and relatively untapped (at least for the time being). The bad boy of the family is Prince Mobile.

Figure 3 outlines not only the prevalence of smartphone use, but also how rapidly it's going to increase by 2016. As more people search for and consume information on the go with their highly functional smartphones, mobile will play an integral role in any successful digital marketing strategy.

Prince Mobile continues to grow and become more prominently featured at the core of digital marketing, which makes him the next King of the Digital Royal Family.

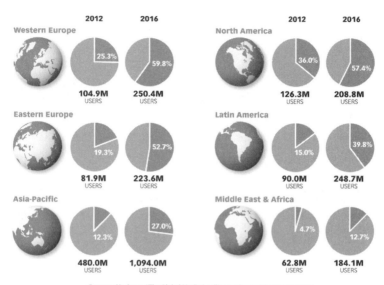

Source: eMarketer, "The Global Media Intelligence Report", September 2012.

Figure 3: Global Media Intelligence Report

Social is Princess

The darling of the Digital Royal Family – the belle of the ball – is Princess Social (short for Social Media – sometimes she drops her middle name). She's cutting edge, not afraid to take risks, and although she's still changing at breakneck speed, businesses can't afford to ignore Princess Social's rapid growth.

Figure 4 shows constant amounts of growth in social networking spend from 2010-2012. In the coming years, social spend is expected to increase by 33%, followed by another 22% the next year. Social media is here to stay. The many businesses that are choosing not to use social – mainly because they don't understand it – are going to regret their refusal to adapt. The key to unlocking the value of social media is embracing it and finding a way to make it work for your business.

Princess Social is poised to transition into her role as the next Queen of the Digital Royal Family. The Social Media chapter will delve a little deeper into how you can successfully integrate Princess Social into your digital marketing efforts.

Social Network Ad Spending Share Worldwide, by Region, 2010-2014
% of total

	2010	2011	2012	2013	2014
North America	55.2%	50.7%	49.7%	48.8%	48.9%
Western Europe	27.4%	25.4%	24.6%	22.3%	20.9%
Asia-Pacific	14.4%	19.4%	20.6%	22.9%	23.7%
Eastern Europe	1.7%	2.3%	2.5%	2.8%	2.8%
Latin America	1.2%	1.9%	2.3%	2.7%	3.1%
Middle East & Africa	0.1%	0.2%	0.3%	0.4%	0.6%

Note: includes display, search, video and other forms of paid advertising appearing within social networks, social games and social applications; excludes spending by marketers that goes toward developing or maintaining social network profile pages or branded applications; numbers may not add up to 100% due to rounding
Source: eMarketer, Nov 2012

147561   www.**eMarketer**.com

Figure 4: Worldwide Social Network Ad Spend Share

Digital Marketing Framework

Now that the Digital Royal Family has been introduced, it's time to take a step back and look at the type of environment your business needs to create in order for them to thrive. Content, advertising, mobile and social media will make up the foundation of your digital marketing efforts, but what kind of base do they have? This base is called a digital marketing framework. The framework is a six-step process, made up of the following phases: Discovery, Internet Business Analysis, Build, Implement, Measure and Manage Results.

Discovery

The first and most important element of the digital marketing framework is Discovery. It's the longest phase and requires the most time and energy to piece together, but if done correctly, it'll ensure the success of the other five phases and drive your entire digital marketing strategy. The core components of Discovery include identifying goals and objectives, selecting strategies and tactics, exploring new opportunities, and setting metrics and targets.

Internet Business Analysis

The second phase of the digital marketing framework is the Internet Business Analysis. Now that your goals and objectives have been identified, the next step is researching how best to implement a digital marketing strategy. There are three specific tasks that will yield valuable information: market segmentation, persona development and competitor analysis.

In the process of market segmentation, a business will consider which pieces of the market to target and then analyze those areas. You'll have much greater success when targeting niches rather than jumping headlong into a vast and uncharted ocean of consumers.

Persona development involves the creation of fictitious characters that represent various types of your customers by incorporating different demographics, interests, locations, age groups, gender and behavior. Once personas are created, specific and more personal campaigns and strategies can be used to target the differing customer types which will lead to a higher conversion rate, more sales and a better ROI.

Before implementing digital marketing tactics, it's a good idea for you to analyze your competitors to see what they're doing in the digital space. An in-depth competitor analysis often returns valuable information including strategies that are working for your competitors (which you can then implement) and areas where you can gain a definite competitive advantage.

Build

The next component of the digital marketing framework is Build. The Build phase is where the strategic development of a digital marketing plan shifts into resource planning and allocation. Before the requirements of a digital marketing strategy can be built or implemented, your business needs to have a discussion about who will build it and at what cost? Are there enough staff members to handle it internally or do you need an agency or consultant? How much budget do you have available?

Businesses that choose to work with consultants will discover that experts can alleviate the pressures of Build (and much of the following three phases) from the equation as they'll already be off and running with the project at this point.

Regardless of the path, the Build phase is where you'll set up or modify your digital assets, which are things like your website, social media profiles and the development of any other digital campaigns.

Implement

Following Build is the Implement phase. During this period all of the digital assets and campaigns tasked throughout Build need to be scheduled for launch and subsequently activated. A cohesive and well-organized launch strategy can pay dividends as it's often an underrated part of most digital marketing efforts.

Measure

Once businesses are fully operating within the digital space, many consider their job done. They sit back and wait for good things to start happening and are either satisfied by mediocre results or simply disappointed. Don't build, implement and wait, because it won't do you any good. The Measure phase of the digital marketing framework is what enables you to determine which strategies work best and enhance those that are generating a positive ROI with your marketing budget.

Since most businesses aren't aware of the Measure phase, this is another area where an agency or consultant can assist. A consultant helps you determine target goals for each digital tactic and then sets up the measurement of those metrics.

Manage Results

The Manage Results phase is the final cog in the digital marketing framework. One of the most helpful aspects of digital marketing is that anything and everything can be measured. After implementing a campaign and letting it run for a reasonable amount of time (and also tracking it correctly), it'll be easy to discern whether the campaign works. If it doesn't, pull the plug. If it works, start the digital marketing framework again and figure out how to enhance it.

Most businesses aren't managing their results - at least not yet. The monitoring of digital marketing efforts allows you to make ongoing adjustments and rapid improvements to campaigns. The Manage Results phase is the key to more efficient digital marketing and could be the competitive edge your business is lacking.

The Benefits of a Process

The digital marketing framework is really a cycle, much like WSI's Digital Marketing Lifecycle™. Adhering to a cyclical process is especially efficient for digital marketing due to the constantly shifting nature of the industry. What works now won't work next year if it isn't updated and adapted to reflect the changes of the Internet, technology, consumer behavior and industry best practices.

WSI's Digital Marketing Lifecycle™ was created as a framework to developing and maintaining successful digital marketing strategies. Each phase works in tandem with the next and is vital to the cycle as a whole. If a segment is left incomplete, the cycle becomes disconnected and the digital components involved will never meet their full potential.

Figure 5: The WSI Lifecycle

First Things First:
The Importance of Discovery

While all phases of the digital marketing framework do play an equal role in the overall success of any digital marketing strategy, there would be no framework without the Discovery phase. Businesses often have a hard time determining how and where to start their digital marketing efforts, and since most are in a hurry to catch up, things can get messy. And a messy start just breeds dysfunction, inefficiency and ultimately failure, which leaves that business – the one that was rushing to get online – even further behind the competition.

Identifying Goals and Objectives

As part of the Discovery phase, you'll need to identify your goals and objectives. For most businesses, these goals and objectives break down into three categories: lead generation, brand awareness and customer retention.

The first step to identifying your goals and objectives is to determine how your current efforts align with these categories and analyze how effective those efforts have been. This analysis should help you expose gaps and areas of opportunity within your strategy, which allows you to begin identifying a new set of goals and objectives for digital marketing campaigns.

Lead generation. The objective of any business is to fill a consumer need with a product, service or solution. However this requires one important thing: actual customers. You might offer an amazing service, but if nobody knows about or realizes its value, it won't succeed. Lead generation is any process or tactic that puts you in front of customers to make them aware of your offerings.

Due to the nature of lead generation – which simply means finding customers – startup businesses and companies without an audience or client base should focus on this process. Digital strategies that excel at lead generation include display advertising, paid search advertising (PPC) and search engine optimization (SEO).

Brand awareness. Of course businesses want more people to be aware of their brand, but many don't know how to proactively enhance consumer knowledge. Brand awareness means ensuring that potential clients are aware of your business and the products you offer. Consider the Kleenex brand, for example. Kleenex is a brand of facial tissue, but many people simply refer to the noun, facial tissue, as Kleenex. *That's* brand awareness.

Kleenex is a big brand, but there are many techniques that can help you increase the rate at which consumers attach your brand's name to a product or service. Content marketing and display advertising are great strategies that, when combined and properly executed, can accomplish an incredible spike in brand awareness.

Customer retention. Keeping customers happy is a hallmark of successful businesses. But the game has changed. Perhaps the most drastic shift brought on by digital marketing and the Internet is the way customers seek out and engage with the brands they purchase. If your brand isn't accessible or willing to interact with customers – on both sides of the buying cycle – you're at risk of losing potential customers and retaining less of your current clientele.

Having an open line of communication with your customers and giving them more access to your business is a great way to foster trust and good will with both prospective and current clients. Content, social and email marketing are very effective strategies you can use to improve your overall ability to retain customers.

Selecting Tactics

Once a business has effectively set its goals and objectives for a digital marketing campaign, the next step is to decide which tactics are best suited to hit specific targets. Many businesses jump into digital without understanding the strengths or purpose of the tactics they attempt to implement, often trying to do a little bit of everything. Doing a little bit of everything is a huge mistake. If you only have the budget and employee time to do a few of these things, it's better to do those few really well than all of them poorly.

Additionally, you need to implement the strategies that best align with your goals. Some tactics do a better job of generating leads, so if leads are a priority, you should devote most of your focus to tactics that excel at lead generation.

Content marketing. Since content is the core of many other digital tactics, content marketing is actually a very balanced and effective strategy in all three categories. Overall, content marketing slightly favors customer retention, but it's still a great way to generate leads and increase brand awareness, and is a vital component of any successful digital strategy.

Paid search advertising (PPC). Paid search advertising (the pay per click ads found on search engine results pages) is an exceptional lead generation tool. To a lesser extent, PPC campaigns can be effective for brand awareness, but they excel at honing in on people who are interested in your product or service and driving them to your website. Again, if customer retention is your main objective, paid search advertising isn't the answer.

Display advertising. Similar to PPC, display advertising is a great lead generation tool for all businesses. But where display advertising excels is in the brand awareness category. Once a customer engages with your brand, the goal is to convert them to a brand advocate so that they recommend and say good things about your product or service. If you're struggling to retain customers however, display advertising isn't the best strategy.

Search engine optimization (SEO). SEO helps direct search engine traffic to websites and is similar to PPC, except there's no charge for these clicks. SEO is a very effective lead generation tool and also helps out in the brand awareness department. By targeting specific keywords, SEO can connect you with searchers who are looking for the products and services you offer.

Social media marketing. Facebook, Twitter, LinkedIn and Google+ are social platforms that many businesses are struggling to incorporate into their marketing plans. And that's understandable. Social media is young and changes very rapidly. But the businesses that have figured out that social media marketing is a valuable component to brand awareness and customer retention are ahead of the curve and reaping the benefits of early adoption. Social can be an invaluable tool for connecting with customers, answering questions about products and services and improving the customer experience.

Video marketing. Much like social and mobile, video marketing has exploded over the last few years. As the cost of creating videos has decreased, it's become an excellent strategy for increasing brand awareness. Video also complements both social and SEO efforts by encouraging consumer engagement and boosting organic rankings. If used correctly, videos can be leveraged for lead generation but overall, they're most effective for expanding your brand and allowing you to creatively market your products and services.

Email marketing. Second to only content marketing in terms of overall balance, email marketing is an incredibly effective and underrated tactic. By remaining top-of-mind and reaching out to your customers, email marketing is great at customer retention and brand awareness. Because of the many ways to collect email addresses – by giving away free content, running contests, and engaging on social media – email marketing can also help you generate leads and make initial contact with potential customers.

Conversion architecture. Landing page optimization and responsive design, which fall under conversion architecture, are vital components of lead generation tactics. If you run PPC and display ad campaigns, you'll need to ensure your website is optimized for conversion to enhance those strategies. Conversion architecture should be implemented to augment lead generation and brand awareness tactics.

Mobile marketing. As smartphone adoption continues to rise and tablets become increasingly popular, more people are searching, engaging and making purchase decisions from their mobile devices. Like social media, mobile is relatively young and most businesses are trying to get a handle on how they can incorporate it. But the truth is, some businesses have mastered mobile and are launching themselves ahead of the competition with it. Mobile is an excellent tactic for brand awareness and customer retention.

Everything Works Together

The purpose of the Discovery phase is to help you invest a relatively small amount of time in return for major results. The time and honesty required to analyze and identify your goals and objectives for digital marketing will pay off. Not only will the Discovery phase give you a clear internal picture with regards to your marketing, but it'll set you up to achieve marketing success where it matters most: on the Internet.

Businesses that want to accomplish total digital marketing success can also become educated on the strategies and techniques they may not know or understand. For example, if you decide to throw a bunch of money at social and mobile marketing, educate your team. If you don't take the time to teach your employees about the strategy and the goals and objectives behind it, the techniques may have a hard time gaining traction. When it comes to digital marketing, the whole team needs to be on-board.

The world of digital marketing can be daunting. Things move and change quickly, and what works today might be dated a few months down the road. As a result, you should consider consulting experts to keep you up to speed on the evolving landscape of the Internet, because when the Internet changes, so does the digital marketing framework. The perfect digital strategies are often a mix of in-house talent and the creativity and knowledge of industry experts, so don't be afraid to think outside the box or ask for help.

2

CONTENT MARKETING IS KING

By Francois Muscat

In the past, businesses could get away with sending their messages in short bursts through traditional marketing mediums. But today, businesses are shifting toward attracting their target market with good content. The importance of quality content has caused many marketers to transform into publishing departments that create and distribute educational and compelling content to their customers. Your business needs to start doing exactly the same thing.

Content marketing has given small businesses the opportunity to become publishers of news and content and has leveled the playing field. Now, even the little guys can publish content. But the challenge that small businesses usually face is finding the time and talent to develop a consistent flow of new and interesting information.

Some marketers believe they can use any type of content to support any type of marketing. And while content marketing makes use of social media, it's different than social media marketing.

Customers expect businesses to have registered social media profiles on Twitter, Facebook and LinkedIn. Social profiles give customers a way to connect with you and ask questions about your products and services. Social profiles also act as platforms for distributing content, which helps build the audience needed to grow and expand your customer base.

When you post high quality content, you're giving potential customers free and useful information (as opposed to hard-selling your offerings). With articles, blog posts, case studies and whitepapers, you can use your expertise to creatively attract and engage an audience and build your brand. Content and social media marketing work in tandem to help increase that audience by distributing links to your high quality content.

Why Business Managers Should Support Content Marketing

When it comes to content marketing, a business needs to focus on its top priorities – lead generation and brand awareness. Content marketing builds your brand's identity in a way that's personable and attractive to millions of Internet users.

The main reason why traditional advertising is no longer enough is that people find the information they need online. Consumers now use the Internet to research a product, company or solution. Content helps you attract people to your products as they relate to solutions offered, not products sold.

A Website Isn't Enough

A static, five page website doesn't build trust or a consumer base. A volume of frequent and useful content drives SEO, which helps businesses rank well on Google. An absence of fresh content leads to poor rankings and no visibility on search engines or other platforms.

Some traditional marketers feel that content marketing is giving away something for free with no return. But by producing content, your business becomes a reliable, trusted source of information, which is then associated with your products. A good reputation is priceless.

Content Marketing Makes Financial Sense

Content marketing takes time and money to produce (whether created in-house or outsourced to a copywriter), but it's extremely cost effective when compared to other online tactics such as display or paid search advertising. You need to look at content marketing as an opportunity to address the largest audience possible. Producing content and distributing it online is like being a keynote speaker at a conference full of potential clients – every single day.

Measurable Interaction and Returns

There are a number of metrics by which the success of a content marketing strategy can be measured. According to 2013 B2B Content Marketing Benchmarks, marketers look at the following things:

Measurement Criteria for B2B Content Marketing Success

Web Traffic — 60%
Sales Lead Quality — 51%
Social Media Sharing — 45%
Sales Lead Quantity — 43%
Direct Sales — 41%
Qualitative Feedback from Customers — 41%
SEO Ranking — 41%
Time Spent on Website — 39%
Inbound Links — 35%
Benchmark Lift of Company Awareness — 26%
Increased Customer Loyalty — 24%
Benchmark Lift of Product/Service Awareness — 22%
Cross-selling — 13%
Cost Savings — 5%

2013 B2B Content Marketing Benchmarks–North America: CMI/MarketingProfs

Figure 6: Measurement Criteria for B2B Content Marketing Success***

Web traffic. The number of visits your website gets is one of the metrics that shows whether you're publishing quality content that people are reading. Analytics programs can determine what people are looking for, how long they stay on certain pages of content, and what they find most useful. This allows you to further tailor your content strategy to ensure that potential customers visit and engage with your website.

Direct sales. While it's great to build a loyal following with a content marketing strategy, the bottom line remains an important part of every business. If you're able to increase your direct sales thanks to publishing useful content, you know you're on the right track.

Sales lead quality. The quality of sales leads is also a great way to measure how well you understand customers. If the content you publish clearly addresses your target market's needs, it will attract quality sales leads.

Qualitative customer feedback. When you start engaging with customers online, you gain the opportunity to ask customers for feedback via a website form, an article, or through comments on social media.

Reaching an Audience with Content Marketing

Customers are online and looking for products, services and solutions to their problems. It's up to you to grab customers first (and make no mistake - the competition from other companies trying to do just that is huge).

Content marketing is about understanding what consumers are searching for and how long they're prepared to look for it.

Create Great Content

In order to start creating the kind of content your customers want to read, follow these five steps:

Understand the challenges customers face. Businesses can't write for everybody – they need to identify a well-defined (and well-understood) group of prospects. This is an area where persona development and targeted persona content can help businesses immensely.

Solve problems. Businesses need to shift the way they market their offerings. Instead of defining the value of products or services as features, you need to focus on the problems that your target audience faces and create content that solves these problems.

Become a trusted source. An important part of content marketing is to become a trusted source of information for target buyers. Businesses should aim to build a loyal following that trusts the information they publish. This only happens when you create meaningful content that helps solve problems.

Write fresh content. Businesses do still need standard content like a five page website with contact details and company history, but they also need to provide timely content at regular intervals. Blog posts are a great way to do this. Creating a blog-powered website can be a huge differentiating factor for small and medium-sized businesses.

Make it easy to buy. Businesses don't have to hard sell, but they need to make it easy for people to transition from interested prospect to paying customer. Online products, contact information and services need to be easily accessible.

Distribute Content Online

Posting and distributing content online gives businesses the opportunity to create more ways for their customers to find, read about and trust them. A content marketing strategy that includes social media marketing creates a campaign-driven, highly strategic plan to track the cause and effect of these efforts through consumer engagement. Measurements like the number of retweets or the amount of people sharing your content show results and drive future campaigns.

The main goals of a content marketing strategy are lead generation and customer retention, which are achieved by sharing free and useful information to create brand awareness and position you as an expert in your field.

Content Marketing is About the Customer

A business's website should be more about its customers and less about the bottom line. If customers can see that you prioritize their needs, they'll trust you and your product, which sets them on their way to becoming an advocate of your brand.

Make Content Personal

Content marketing gives businesses a unique platform on which to address clients personally and casually. You can be more fun and get creative with these interactions since you aren't limited the way you are with other types of advertising.

Build Search Personas

Most businesses have more than one target audience and need to create content for each potential buyer. A good starting point when planning a content strategy is to identify the top three to five personas that are likely to visit your website. Think about each of these personas in terms of the information they'd want to access from your website, and help them make the decision to use your products or services. Tailor your content towards the kind of people who are most likely to visit your website.

Consider the groups of people who buy from a paint company: handy household owners on a budget, small or large contractors, and artists. What would their concerns be and how would they differ? What do they want from the paint they buy? These questions provide answers that the paint company can use to attract potential clients that are looking for a solution rather than a product. The paint company could create content with titles such as: "How to Paint Wooden Furniture" or "What Paint Products Are Best for Industrial Buildings?"

SEO, or more specifically, the use of relevant keywords to create and optimize compelling content is an important part of an effective content strategy. But first you need to take a step back and determine what techniques align with your customers' needs. Create search personas to better understand what your customers are searching for online. Use these steps to build search personas:

Define your ideal customer. Businesses should be able to pinpoint their ideal customer. If you own a business that sells paint, you know your target market is relatively hands-on in terms of building and renovating, and they're more likely to be men aged 25 – 45.

Understand customers' problems and challenges. How would your customers articulate their pain points? What type of keywords would they be typing into search engines? A man looking for paint may search for "exterior paint" or "easy to clean interior paint", for example.

Create great content. You need to create great content that's optimized for these search phrases. Your content also needs to offer a solution, such as a call to action that will enable the reader to contact you for more information or to buy the product immediately.

Intrigue the reader. It's not easy to convert a searcher into a customer on a single page, so focus on calls to action that compel the reader to dive further into your sales funnel. Keep writing pages that are relevant to your searchers and drill down into things that are interesting and relevant to them.

Next, determine which social networks your potential customers are on. Younger, less formal searchers use Facebook, Twitter and Pinterest, while professionals are more likely to use LinkedIn. These are the social media profiles you need to create in order to distribute your content to the right people and build your customer base.

Channel Potential Buyers

If there's one thing that frustrates readers, it's reading content they're not particularly interested in while trying to find a solution to their problem. Channel your potential buyers directly to relevant content by asking them exactly why they're on your site.

For example, allow website visitors to select the content channel they prefer by having a clear site structure, easy navigation and proper content segmentation. This helps readers avoid content they have no interest in and guides them to relevant areas of your website more efficiently.

You can also enable a reader to relate to your content immediately by using customer testimonials and case studies. These are both perfect ways to show your potential clients that your product is as high quality as your marketing media suggests.

Use Marketing Funnels

The marketing funnel is a model that follows the journey of how a potential customer becomes a client. Planning and creating a funnel helps you determine exactly how you can streamline the sales process of your company.

This model will help ensure that you don't miss out on the most significant audience – the people who are looking for a solution, but aren't yet aware that your company can provide it. The best way to achieve this is to publish educational blogs, articles and social media links parallel to your product and services. These should try to address reasons that potential clients could come into contact with your company. Here are the steps of a marketing funnel:

Step one. In the first stage, potential buyers have a query about something they're looking for but may not know where to find relevant information or what product they actually require. People use search engines and social sites to help them find what they're looking for, which hopefully leads them to your business's website and social profiles.

Step two. A buyer's next step is to do further research on your products with more in-depth information like eBooks, webinars and industry reports in order to make an informed decision. Your case studies and customer testimonials provide corroborating material to reassure potential clients that your product and service is their best choice.

Step three. Lastly, detailed product information and analyst reports tell the potential client exactly how to use your product upon purchase.

This model helps you address and hold your potential client's attention from the very beginning of the process, allowing them to navigate through your content and move towards a purchase while empowering them with relevant information at each stage of the buying process.

The Importance of Content Marketing

- The Internet is the go-to tool for initial research – if you aren't there, you don't exist to many potential customers
- Staying power – the right kind of content is relevant for many years
- You get to communicate directly with your customers
- Content that is closely related to your product will attract new clients when they search for their needs rather than specific products
- Tell your customers about your expertise in the industry, where you're going and what you're planning so that you become a trusted advisor and strategic partner

Content Marketing Tactics

There are many different types of content. Here are just a few ideas:

Social media. Use social networks to distribute links to content rather than posting the content itself. Answer product questions by linking to quality content.

Articles. Articles put your brand and product in the public eye. They also help you come across as an expert in your field and give your brand and products credibility.

Events. Distribute relevant, interesting content at trade shows and conferences. Draw people to your website properties by putting quick response (QR) codes on brochures and letting them know where they can ask you questions online (your social media profiles).

Blogs. Blogs give you a personal connection with your customers and provide you with the opportunity to give more detail than you'd be able to give on Facebook or Twitter.

Webinars. Create interactive conferences that allow you to train or educate people over the Internet (you could even broadcast a presentation on how to use your product). A name, face and a voice lend credibility to what you're saying.

Images. Content marketing isn't just text and video. Images, such as infographics, can be combined with your text to provide information-rich eye-candy for readers. Images can also attract search engine browsers and make your article or blog stand out from the crowd.

Content calendar. Create a content calendar to make sure your potential customers are receiving relevant material at regular intervals. It allows you to schedule and organize material for blogs and social networks well in advance. This way you ensure that your Twitter and Facebook posts coincide with relevant blog posts. A content calendar that includes all your posting platforms helps potential clients move through social media along a clearly defined path that addresses their specific need.

Achieving Content Marketing Success

There are a few things businesses can do to ensure a content marketing strategy is successful. These are the qualities of a successful content marketing campaign:

- Well-written, high quality content
- Have something new to say and ensure your content is well researched
- Understand your target market and provide information people are looking for
- Give your target audience something they haven't seen before
- Do keyword research and create targeted content
- Your content needs to be personal because you need your consumers to like and trust you
- Be interesting and engaging by using videos, product reviews, podcasts and eBooks to add variety and creative flair to your content strategy
- Allow comments on your articles, blogs and social media to initiate two-way conversations
- Organize your publishing plan with an editorial calendar

Make Content Marketing Work for You

You can't do everything yourself, so assign a small team to handle content marketing for your company. Do intense research to determine which content marketing tactics work best for you.

Content marketing doesn't have to be limited to two or three people. Encourage participation from outside the marketing team – remember that you're trying to figure out what people from all walks of life want to know about your product. The people within your company have probably been asked many questions about your products that have never been addressed to a wider audience. These questions will help you generate content ideas that need to be researched. Similarly, if clients are contacting you with questions, chances are there are hundreds of people online that are asking the same thing. If you can answer these questions with interesting content, you've implemented a winning content marketing strategy.

Once you've got content ideas and people assigned to create content, set targets so that the team knows how many blog posts and social media updates need to be posted within a specific timeframe. Keep in mind that the backbone of successful content marketing is a consistent flow of new and interesting information. Lastly, use analytics programs to see how well you're doing and in what ways you can improve, add to and streamline your content marketing strategy.

3

PPC: GET LEADS FAST

By Benjamin Smith

Paid search advertising (pay-per-click or PPC) are ads placed in search engines. PPC ads appear on search engine results pages (SERPS) above and to the right of the organic web listings. The positioning of PPC ads is determined by a keyword bidding process. Google refers to PPC as search marketing and their ad platform is called AdWords. Other search engines, notably Bing and Yahoo, also offer PPC ad systems.

PPC involves placing ads on SERPs that link to one of your website pages. When a searcher clicks on your ad, they're directed to the corresponding page. The process begins with a silent auction for keywords (search terms) relevant to your business that, along with what Google calls the quality score of your ad, determines the placement of your ad within the listings. Quality Score is determined by the keyword's click through rate (CTR) on Google, relevance of ad text, historical keyword performance, landing page keyword focus, and other relevancy factors. Each keyword must be bid on individually and can be associated with an ad group containing variations of the advertising message all with a link to one of your website pages.

So what's more valuable to businesses: SEO or PPC? The truth is, it depends on factors like:

- How competitive the keywords that are relevant to your business are
- The cost of PPC bids for various keywords
- Whether your business is local, regional or national
- The type and cost of product or service you market
- How much time you can budget to the PPC and SEO administrative tasks
- How many leads you need to either maintain or expand your business

There are several important aspects of paid search advertising, including:

- Keyword research
- Well-crafted ad copy
- A/B ad testing
- Bid management with multiple publishers
- Landing page content relevance
- Call to action strategy
- Results measurement

Quick and Reliable Traffic for a Fixed Cost

Paid search is a unique form of advertising in the sense that it provides immediate results. Ads properly managed can appear quickly on page one of a SERP, unlike organic website listings that take a long time to reach page one, if ever.

Quite literally, a PPC ad can be written, published, and on its way to driving results for your company before you even finish reading this chapter. It can be turned off just as quickly. Furthermore, ads can be scheduled in advance and turned on and off on specific dates and times.

For example, imagine that you're a car dealer and the manufacturer just started a major television advertising campaign for a new car model that you sell. Since you want to leverage the increased interest created by the commercials, you quickly setup a PPC ad specifically for that model. You set the campaign to only target searches in the city where your dealership is located and direct the traffic to the page on your website about that car model. Local search traffic immediately starts flowing to that page where customers can view available inventory and connect with a salesperson.

Reliable Traffic

You'd agree that when an advertising method is driving positive results to your business, you hope it continues day after day. That just so happens to be one of the major benefits of PPC marketing.

There are billions of searches completed every day on search engines and there's no end in sight for the growth in search volume. Many of the searches are for specific products or services, a portion of which are probably very relevant for almost every business.

With the right keyword mix, it's not difficult to maintain a steady stream of reliable traffic to your website. Each day brings new customers to your website, all searching specifically for the product or service you provide.

Are you a home improvement contractor, a mechanic, or maybe a local restaurant? Perhaps you're a regional distributor of commercial appliances, or a national manufacturer of packaging supplies. Imagine all the customers searching for your products and services right now, but going to your competitors instead. Imagine if they could be your customers tomorrow, and the day after that, and the day after that! That's what PPC can do for your business.

Fixed Cost

With a dynamic, auction based pricing system you might think PPC advertising costs fluctuate unpredictably from month to month. But actually, that's hardly the case when a PPC campaign is setup correctly.

The search engines provide you with tools to limit settings for cost per click and daily budgets. What this allows you as the advertiser to do is provide a cost ceiling and create a fairly predictable monthly advertising budget. Keyword bids and placement will be automatically adjusted to fit your set budget by the PPC ad platform.

To take this a step further, there are many third-party tools available to integrate with search engines that allow cost and budget controls to be even more precise than those controls provided directly by the search engines.

Bid optimization platforms offer several advantages. For example, keyword bid adjustment best practices can be a bit of a tedious task to complete. That's where bid optimization software comes into play. These types of tools monitor bids and activity, and adjust individual keyword bids to remain competitive or fit within your budget.

Oftentimes bid optimization tools can even be set to target a desired cost per lead or cost per product sold. With the right feedback mechanisms in place, these tools can help deliver a very reliable and consistent cost per acquisition.

For instance, a dental practice looking for new patients might be willing to spend $100 to acquire a new lifetime client. With some understanding about PPC best practices, an optimization platform will experiment with keywords, bids, and placement so that $100 average per lead is maintained.

These systems will also learn which keywords are more likely to drive traffic that converts into customers. Over time, the optimization algorithms will begin to focus more of your budget on those keywords. That way you're always receiving the most value for your PPC spend.

This type of optimization combined with a set monthly budget creates a predictable fixed cost for PPC.

Target Keywords That Are Difficult to Rank For

Ads reach a target demographic (location, interests, income, age, etc) via selected keywords, bids, and ad settings within the publisher's ad platform.

A high organic search engine ranking via SEO is the gold standard, but that's an overwhelming task to achieve for a multitude of keywords as each keyword needs a top ranked website page and the web presence for each keyword needs to be extensive. With PPC there is no overwhelming barrier to the number of keywords with a high-ranking search engine ad; all that is needed is an optimized landing page for each keyword and a sufficient budget for the ad.

So a practical approach to search marketing is to prioritize a limited number of keywords for SEO top organic ranking, then supplement with PPC advertising to dominate search engine listings for priority keywords. That way you'll create a multi-position search engine presence for high priority keywords plus gain coverage for a multitude of lower priority keywords.

You also don't have to worry so much about how long it'll take you to naturally rank for a competitive term. As long as you are properly managing your PPC, you'll quickly be listed on page one.

Laser Target Ads

A properly setup PPC campaign will contain ads that are extremely relevant to the specific product or service you're trying to promote. More searchers will be converted into customers if your keywords, ad text, and landing page work in harmony.

Writing specific ads that properly target the intended audience will improve your performance tremendously. You can use your ad text as a door man, directing qualified customers to your website. This is important since you don't want to pay for a click on your ad unless there's a good chance it'll turn into a customer.

General search terms are called 'short tail' keywords and are usually one or two words long. Specific search terms are called 'long tail' keywords that are usually three or more words long. For competitive reasons, it's costly to rank high for short tail keywords, but easier with lower cost per click for niche long tail keywords.

Let's use home mortgage loans as an example. Sure, there are many searches for home loans as a general term, but a customer in the buying cycle is searching for something much more specific. He's searching for a fixed-rate 30-year mortgage, a five-year ARM loan, a 5% down home loan, or home refinance with low APR.

These specific search terms combined with an ad that specifically speaks to that search will engage the searcher at a higher rate. When that searcher clicks on an ad and is directed to a website page that gives him specific details about the type of loan he searched, you've set up the best possible scenario to obtain a new customer.

Furthermore, a nationwide bank with many locations in specific cities should also target ads geographically. A person searching for a loan will be even more comfortable clicking on an ad if it mentions their specific city.

Remember, you only have seconds to convince a searcher that they should click on your ad. You want to make it as obvious as possible that a searcher will find exactly what they're looking for if they choose to visit your site.

Mobile Search is Vital for Local Businesses

Mobile search simply refers to a search done on a mobile phone. A large portion of locals searching via mobile device 'walk through the door' and a big chunk of that foot traffic ends up buying something.

If you're a local business that relies on people visiting you in order to make a sale, then you're among the group of advertisers that can benefit the most from the increasing use of mobile search.

According to a study by AT&T Interactive and Nielsen, the most mobile searched for businesses are:[1]

- Restaurants
- Entertainment Venues
- Retail Shops
- Grocery
- Travel
- Automotive
- Health and Beauty

The CTR for mobile ads is extremely high:[2]

- Ad for a trusted brand = 36% CTR
- Ad for a deal or coupon = 33% CTR
- Ad for an item close to what was searched for = 31% CTR

(Note that the CTR for Computer based PPC ads or banner ads is typically <2%)

These types of businesses can extensively leverage local PPC traffic, because they can target people using their mobile phones. Due to the growth of mobile connectivity, Google recently upgraded its AdWords platform to make it easier to differentiate and manage PPC ads aimed at various devices.

AdWords Enhanced Campaigns

Google recently launched an update to AdWords that includes the capability to increase keyword bids when someone is searching within a close radius of a business's location.

AdWords Enhanced Campaigns are designed to help make PPC campaigns more efficient by expanding them across the many platforms people use to search (PCs, smartphones and tablets). Before, AdWords revolved around searcher intent; with Enhanced Campaigns, your ads capture intent and context.

For example, a sushi restaurant probably wants to target searchers within 5 miles of the restaurant during the dinner rush. With Enhanced Campaigns, the sushi place can launch a single campaign that reaches all devices and increase bids by 25% for customers who are searching on a smartphone 5 miles from the restaurant between 5pm-8pm, or decrease bids by 30% during hours they're closed. Enhanced Campaigns give the sushi restaurant a better opportunity to grab customers who are nearby and hungry!

Even better, Google ads show your address and phone number so customers can easily get directions or call you for a reservation without even clicking through to your site.

Measurable Results Equals Increased Conversion

As soon as a PPC campaign is launched, businesses can begin collecting data. Not only can you simply track number of impressions and visits, but you can also track conversions in several different ways. A conversion is defined by the advertiser, for example: a sale, a subscription, a contact, a download or whatever goal the advertiser is trying to achieve with the ad. Smart marketers will then use that data to make improvements in PPC campaigns.

Track Individual Ads and Test New Ones

Within the reporting systems of search engines, it's very easy to check the performance of ads and how well they convert search traffic into customers. The most important metrics to monitor are an ad's CTR and conversion rate – the higher the better.

It's not always easy to predict what ad text is going to drive the most new customers, so the best practice is to continually experiment with new ads. You can even run multiple ads at the same time and see which one works better. This practice is called A/B testing. Frankly, if you're not testing, you're likely leaving money on the table.

Sometimes just one or two words make a difference, so always test variations of ad titles, special offers, and calls to action. Tell people exactly what they'll get if they click on your ad, and give them a reason to click on yours and not your competitor's. In general, the ad should contain keyword related product or service, an offer or benefit, and a call to action. While ad text space is limited, experienced copywriters can optimize results utilizing A/B testing.

Track Keyword Performance

After you have setup your keywords, monitor the available keyword reports to determine which ones are driving converting traffic. Get rid of the keywords that don't produce results and focus your efforts more on the keywords that are working.

Also, keep an eye open for new keyword opportunities that are revealed in the search logs in your PPC account. You'll find additional, more specific keywords people are actually using to find your ad instead of the broader terms on your keyword list. Add those more granular search terms to your list to see your CTR go up and costs go down.

Not only should you add new keywords, but also add negative keywords. Your negative keyword list should contain words that you do not want to trigger your ad. For example, a sporting goods retailer may bid on a term such as 'dome tent'. There could be people searching for a 'wedding tent' who are obviously not relevant to your business, so be sure to add 'wedding' to your negative keyword list.

When measuring keyword effectiveness, again, CTR and conversion rate are two of the most important factors. However, conversion rate measuring takes a couple of extra steps.

Conversion Tracking

What is important to you when someone actually goes ahead and visits your website through a PPC ad? What exactly are you trying to accomplish? Are you trying to get someone to fill out a form, request an appointment or join your mailing list? Do you have a brochure or white-paper you'd like people to download? Maybe you want someone to pick up the phone and call you.

These are all forms of website conversions that should be tracked individually. You can't fix what you don't measure.

It's normally not difficult to implement, but website conversion tracking usually requires your web developer to insert some snippets of code on various pages of your website to provide feedback to the PPC platform. However, once this code is in place, you'll be able to track the number of web forms that are filled out from PPC traffic, sales, profit, and how many coupons were downloaded.

PPC management platforms are sophisticated enough to trace these conversions back to specific ads and keywords. You'll have all of the data you need to determine what keywords and ads in your campaign are resulting in conversions and which ones are not.

Phone Call Tracking

Not only can businesses track conversions of different events that happen on their website pages, they can also track phone calls resulting from PPC ads.

One of the ways that Google allows you to track phone calls is by providing "click-to-call" tracking numbers that you can use in your ads. When someone places a call using those numbers, the call can be tracked as a conversion from your ad. You'll know right away how effective your ads are at driving phone calls and can make improvements on your PPC strategy to increase call volume.

Just as you can track your calls directly from your Google ad, you can also track and record phone calls once customers land on your site. With third-party phone call tracking tools, calls that come from a customer that arrived at your site through PPC can be tracked separately from your normal phone calls. These calls can be attributed to specific keywords in your PPC campaigns as well and used in optimization of your campaign.

Gain Knowledge and Insight

The whole time a PPC campaign is providing increased revenue to businesses, they can also learn about how to be more efficient by gaining insight into their popular products and services.

Popular Products and Services

One of the most overlooked benefits of running a PPC campaign is knowledge gain. PPC advertising also functions as market research by giving you insights on the most popular search terms people are using to arrive at your site.

Online retailers, for example, should expand their keyword list and experiment with a vast cross section of their products. Some products that haven't sold well in the past might turn out to be very popular with enough search volume.

Insurance companies that traditionally specialize in car insurance might want to test ads about boat insurance or travel insurance. If testing of those niches results in a favorable amount of searches and website traffic, those insurance companies might consider expanding their expertise and offering those types of insurances. Google provides a keyword research tool to help businesses with this kind of experimentation.

Customer Demographics

PPC also offers customer demographic insights that wouldn't otherwise be available offline.

Relevant information, especially for national campaigns, is which geographic locations generate the most customers. If you're a retailer with online sales in addition to brick and mortar stores, you can use PPC to help determine what areas of the country are ripe for new store locations.

PPC also helps you find out what time of day customers are looking for the services you provide. For instance, a cruise travel agency might find that most of its PPC traffic is converting on Monday and Friday nights between 6:30-8:30 pm. They can increase their bids on popular search terms only during those hours, and schedule more customer service agents to handle the higher volume of phone calls.

Phone Call Tracking and Recording

A major side benefit of tracking phone calls for PPC optimization is that you can listen to the recordings. Reviewing calls is a great way to learn about your customers and their needs through the conversations they have with your staff or agents.

Not only can this help you learn more about the products and services your callers are looking for, but customer service improvements can be made as well. The phone recordings can be used for coaching of staff and receptionists to improve the conversion rate of valuable phone leads.

There's Always Room for PPC

Paid search advertising is an essential part of digital marketing and there's room for it in every business's strategy. The nuts and bolts of PPC include:

- Knowledge is power – learn PPC strategies and system administration. Become Google AdWords certified or find a consultant who is certified

- Do keyword research, do keyword research, do keyword research
- Consider using an ad platform that semi-automates multiple publisher bid and ad management
- Learn PPC ad content best practices, create multiple ads for keywords, and do periodic A/B testing to determine ad effectiveness
- Learn how to use PPC related analytics to drive continuous improvement
- Learn how to create effective landing pages (content, layout, colors, images, offers, calls to action) and do periodic A/B testing of landing pages to optimize conversion effectiveness
- Landing pages must be highly relevant to the ad's keyword and message or the ad's quality score will suffer thus affecting ad position and cost

Paid search advertising is a journey, not a destination. The key to running successful PPC campaigns is remaining diligent in learning, researching, planning, implementing, testing, measuring, improving, and then repeating the whole process over again.

4

LANDING PAGE OPTIMIZATION: IT'S ABOUT PSYCHOLOGY NOT TECHNOLOGY

By Chuck Bankoff

"Advertising is the art of getting people to buy things they don't need with money they don't have." This statement predates the Internet by a number of decades, yet still rings true today. While it might be a bit cynical, let's not forget that in the Internet world people rarely stumble across a website without actively searching for something. If you have what people are looking for, it's your job to help them find it.

The problem is most websites are so ill conceived and poorly constructed that they're little more than monuments to their owners.

Let's make something transparently clear; people do not read on the Internet, they scan. They see headlines, images and bullet points. Depending on the personality type of your visitor, you have between two and eight seconds to convince them to stay on your website. Searchers click in, take a quick peak, and click out. Those are the conditions in which business is conducted on the Internet.

What is a Landing Page?

A Landing page is where visitors arrive after clicking on an email link, a search engine result, a banner ad, a PPC ad, or following an offline advertisement like a newspaper, billboard, or TV/radio broadcast.

The objective is to convert the presumably interested consumer into an actual customer by influencing them to take specific action. That action might be downloading a whitepaper in exchange for their contact information, to influence them to spread the word virally, to have them pick up the phone and contact your organization, or the ultimate objective: make an online purchase.

Types of Landing Pages

There are essentially three general categories of landing pages. The choice of which is largely dependent on the specific strategy and goal of the campaign:

Standalone landing pages. These are typical of specific promotions or specific products or services.

On-site landing pages. These often include the homepage or service or product pages.

Microsites. These are typically small multi-page websites with a single focus and a built in sales funnel.

Sub-Types of Landing Pages

Each of the three main landing pages comes in multiple flavors:

Teaser pages. The objective of a teaser page is to give the visitor just enough information to click through to the next stage in the sales cycle. An important aspect of this type of page is to stay on topic by controlling the choices the consumer has and sending them on a predetermined path. To do this, you want to minimize any unnecessary distractions. With each click they essentially qualify themselves as a potential customer. Anyone who doesn't progress to the next step is probably not fit to be your customer. Keep in mind, however, that it may also be an indication that you didn't do a good job teasing them along to the next step, or your traffic to the landing page just wasn't targeted enough.

Squeeze pages. The objective of a squeeze page is to capture the contact information of the visitor to harvest the lead at a later time or as part of a scheduled lead nurturing strategy. An example of lead nurturing might be setting up a series of pre-written emails that are automatically sent to the consumer over a period of weeks, building up interest and culminating in a sales pitch or special offer.

Anyone with common sense understands that once they give up their contact information they're in essence inviting you to sell them something. Therefore you have to barter with them for their personal information by trading something of value, like exclusive information in a whitepaper, access to a webinar, or a discount or coupon not available anywhere else.

A well-designed squeeze page typically has one objective and no navigation or links to other pages. Just gather their data, give them what they bought in exchange for their contact information, and let them go. You'll have plenty of opportunity to reengage them on your terms now that you have their contact info.

Infomercial landing pages. These come in a couple of different flavors, but you've probably seen the ones that resemble the old style sales letter that is mostly text and sensationalism. Just like the classic late night infomercials on TV, they try to verbally make their case as to why you can't live without their product or service. They typically scroll in perpetuity punctuated only by periodic offers you can opt-in to and thus put yourself out of your pain by succumbing to their offer.

A well-designed infomercial landing page is so engaging that you find yourself past the point of no return. The consumer eventually invests so much effort into following the narrative that they're on pins and needles just waiting for the offer. These pages are typically very tightly targeted to a specific market niche.

Viral landing pages. The goal of viral landing pages extends past merely converting your visitors into customers by enlisting them to tell their friends as well. It might be a funny video or a game that is somehow branded to your company via a subtle logo or product placement as part of a greater branding campaign.

It might be a more aggressive incentive based strategy like contests or rewarding accomplishments. Unlike your typical viral video that's fueled by humor or shock value, commercially viral landing pages are powered by incentive. For example, a cloud based service like Dropbox might offer additional storage space if you get a specific number of your friends to join through your tracking link.

> Good viral landing pages have three things in common:

> *Great content.* It doesn't matter how much money or effort you put into the campaign, if you don't have the goods, nobody cares.

> *Incentive.* Give something away, such as additional storage space or a free sample. Or it could be as simple as being the one who found this terrific piece of content and increased your social credibility by sharing it.

> *Convenience.* Sharing your content is inversely proportional to how difficult it is to share. Anyone can copy and paste a link and email it to their friends, but that would require the incentive to be that much richer. One click links like social sharing buttons (share on Twitter, Facebook, Google+, etc)

are a great example of making it easy for consumers to play along.

Figure 7: Social Icons

Microsites. Yes, the Cadillac of landing pages because it requires a bit more commitment. This is essentially a mini-website with its own URL and custom design. These are often the destination of choice for larger investments in the form of paid advertising such as PPC, and print and TV ads.

Despite the fact that they consist of multiple pages, they're typically focused on a single product (or product line). You often see these promoting a movie release or new car model. Obviously microsites often have a limited shelf life as the movie runs its course and the car becomes last year's model.

However some durable goods or "evergreen" products may have a longer shelf life worthy of long-term promotions. In some cases the microsite may even be refreshed along with product updates and special promotions. Just like a successful single landing page, the basic template can be repurposed across multiple product lines.

Product specific landing pages. This is a very common and useful type of landing page because it probably already exists. Typically just an existing page on your website that contains all the information on a specific product or service.

The advantage is that since it's part of your full website, consumers are also free to wander around the site and be exposed to your other products and services. The disadvantage is that consumers are free to wander around your site and be exposed to your other products and services (it's a paradox!). These types of landing pages are certainly convenient, but have a tendency to be unfocused (due to the normal distractions of navigation and links and banners, etc) and harder to track conversions.

Homepage. Typically has the lowest conversion rate because the home page is like the index in a book. It's the jump-off point for the entire contents of the rest of the site. As such, it's unfocused by nature.

However, there are ways around this. For example, employing an eye-catching graphic or headline that's consistent with the message that got the visitor to the site in the first place, thus preserving the continuity of the sales funnel.

The Case for Conversions

It's easy to fall into the trap of throwing money into driving traffic and living with your conversion rate. But the notion that buying traffic means more customers isn't efficient or cost effective.

The scenario below illustrates that a mere 2% increase in conversion results in 240 additional customers without increasing traffic. Depending on the lifetime value of new customers, a 2% conversion increase could be a game changer for businesses.

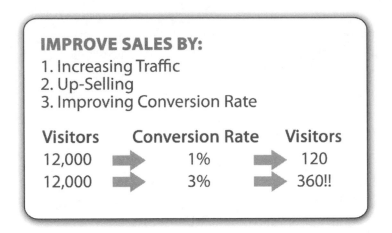

Figure 8: Improve Sales

Tips for Effective Landing Page Design

So what does an effective landing page look like? The simple answer is it can look however you want it to, as long as it contains some important and necessary elements. Here's a list of tips to creating an effective landing page and making it your own.

Define Success

In order to accomplish your goals, you have to know what they are. Is this an eCommerce website focused on transactions? Is the purpose to generate leads, or is it about branding, relationship building, or increasing your database through membership registration? A good marketer will often start at the bottom of the sales funnel and work their way up to the point where the visitor first enters the funnel.

Figure 9: Sales Funnel

Define Your Customer

It's not about you. Many businesses feel compelled to tell their story to what they perceive as a captive audience.

But there's no captive audience on the Internet. Check your ego at the door, it's just too easy for a visitor to leave and find what they really want.

A tried and true technique for defining your customer is to actually create a persona, complete with name, age, marital status and anything else relevant to your target audience. You may even have multiple profiles; just make sure that you prioritize them. Remember, if you try to appeal to too many different customer types, you'll wind up appealing to no one. Once you know who your ideal customer is, you can craft your message so that it appeals to them.

Selecting Domains

Most businesses consider their homepage their landing page. That may be perfectly acceptable in some instances, but it's not always the best choice. Your landing page may be part of a microsite or single page with its own domain name. You might consider one or more "vanity names" targeting a specific product or service. That's particularly effective when the domain will be visible such as on printed material or PPC ads.

Wireframing

A wireframe is a sketch of a page layout. Start by listing all of the elements that go on the page and lay them out on a piece of paper. You should do this before you write the copy because the space available will dictate the amount of copy you have to work with. Make sure that you place the most important elements above the fold (the spot on the page where most visitors will have to scroll down to see more).

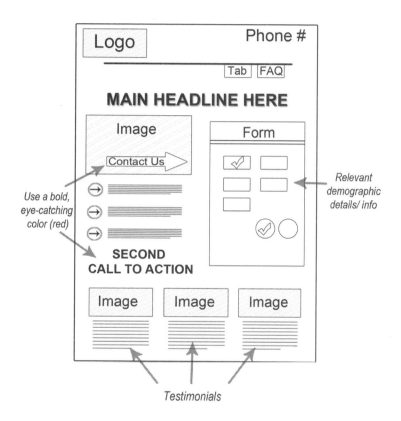

Figure 10: Landing Page Wireframe

Copywriting

As mentioned before, people don't read on the Internet, they scan. They see headlines, bullet points and graphics. It's important your headline refer back to what the visitor was looking at before they landed on your page. Only about 20% of your visitors will actually read the body copy (but that still has to be good).

Don't forget the call to action! You might test matching the call to action with the headline since that's almost certainly the one element on the page that you can be sure people will read.

Testing and Tweaking

This isn't a spare time activity. It's something that should be scheduled at regular intervals. Examine your metrics, make incremental changes and re-examine the effect. Don't make too many changes at once or you won't know what you did to effect the changes. Your testing and adjustments should match your original goals (transactions, lead generation, branding and education, relationship building, registrations, viral marketing).

Elements of a Landing Page

So how many elements need to be on a landing page? The correct answer is as many as necessary, no more and no less.

These are just some items that may go on a landing page. It's not meant to be a checklist of items that should be on every landing page:

- Logo
- Conversion Button
- Offer Explanation
- Headline
- Links to More Information
- Deadlines
- Descriptive Tagline
- Testimonials
- Technical Specifications
- Guarantees
- Rich Media

Copy Tips

- Use half the copy that you would use in printed material
- Headline should match the headline that got them there
- Nothing more than needed, nothing less than needed
- Don't waste valuable real estate with "welcome…"
- "You" and "your" trumps "we" and "our"
- People only read the first few words of bullets and paragraphs
- People read the beginning and end of lists, not the middle
- Keep your first few paragraphs short and inviting
- Alternate long and short paragraphs
- Paragraphs shouldn't be longer than four or five lines

- Numerals have more impact than written numbers

Campaign Killers

Too much text. As mentioned multiple times, people don't read, they scan. They see images, headlines and bullet points. You have 2-8 seconds before they decide to bounce off the page or spend some time on it. How much is the right amount of text? No more or no less than you need to make your case.

Error pages, broken links and anything that does not work. Nothing diminishes confidence like a website that doesn't work. Even worse for landing pages because unlike a website with multiple paths, a landing page has a very specific path down the sales funnel. Anything broken on the path becomes a dead-end.

Required fields. Consumers don't like giving up their personal info for fear of finding themselves on yet another list. Unless you're using required information to pre-screen submissions (where the cost of screening exceeds the value of capturing contact information) you're more likely to get a submission if you try to gather only the most essential information. There will be plenty of time to request their personal information and telephone numbers once you have their basic information and have established a relationship with them. As a general rule, the less you ask for, the more you'll get.

Reset buttons. Have you ever intentionally used a reset button? Have you ever gotten so lost in filling out a simple form that you just give up and reset the entire form? No, of course not. At best a reset button is useless. At worst, a consumer may inadvertently click on it instead of the submit button and delete everything they just filled in. It's hard enough to get them to fill it in the first time, what are the chances they'll fill it in a second time?

No email privacy information next to the email form. Few people actually read a lengthy privacy policy, but most consumers are comforted when you do have one. The mistake is burying it deep on the page when you should be linking to it right at the point where they make the decision whether to submit your form.

Lack of communication choices. Everyone has their favorite communication preference. Some people like to talk with a human being on the phone, some people like live chat because of the spontaneity and anonymity at the same time. Others like the convenience of just filling out a form and shifting the initiative to follow-up to the merchant. There is statistical evidence that having a phone number as an option actually increases form submission simply because of the additional confidence that the merchant is accessible if necessary.

Inadequate shipping and pricing information. No one likes surprises when it comes to money. Not making it clear what a consumer's final price will be (including shipping and taxes) is a sure formula for abandonment.

Too many links leading to too many destinations. Every parent learns that you don't ask a child what they want for breakfast. You ask them if they want Cheerios or Oatmeal. You manage their choices. If you give them too many distractions they wander off the path. Keep it simple and keep it focused.

In-House vs. Outsource

The biggest obstacle to in-house landing page optimization is a lack of resources. In mid-sized companies the marketing department is typically overloaded. In smaller companies the owner or the staff, even if they had the right credentials is (or should be) too busy minding the core business.

Resources. It's tempting to try and do things yourself or assign it to existing staff. Take into consideration the true cost of doing it in-house. Are you diverting staff members from other necessary duties? Are you paying them to learn on the job when an agency or consultant may already have the know-how? You may indeed have the talent under your own roof; just carefully consider the true costs.

Aptitude. Most individuals are either left brained or right brained. That is to say technically or creatively inclined. Since a landing page campaign is a combination of creative and analytical, a technical oriented team or individual isn't likely to come up with the compelling creative, and the creative team may not be able to interpret the data. That applies to agencies as well as you and your staff.

Experience. Agencies may have strengths in both creative and analytics, however they may not have the full array of skill sets necessary to do it any better than you can in-house. Consider the traffic to your landing page.

If your current levels of web traffic are insufficient, make sure you work with a consultant that can deliver everything that you need, either in full or in conjunction with your in-house team.

Summary. Landing pages are unique in that they are generally tied directly to a greater marketing campaign that undoubtedly represents a significant investment for your company. This is not the place to drop the ball and hand the assignment over to whoever has time to deal with it.

Landing page design is a marketing assignment that employs a great deal of psychology. A common mistake companies make is to assign the design of a landing page to their IT department or even their graphics department as a side job when it should be a focal point of their current marketing campaign.

This chapter is not designed as a step-by-step handbook, but rather as a reality check for CEOs and business owners who are about to make an investment in their companies growth and profit.

25-Point Landing Page Checklist

✓ Does your headline say what the page is about and relate to your PPC ad?

✓ Does your sub-headline further refine your message?

✓ Is your landing page focused on a single purpose?

✓ Could someone understand the message in 5-10

seconds?

- ✓ Does the visitor understand what they will get in exchange for contacting you?

- ✓ Does the copy focus on benefits rather than features?

- ✓ Are you using a unique image that tells the story? (No generic stock photos.)

- ✓ Do you have an obvious call to action?

- ✓ Does your landing page look professional?

- ✓ Is your opt-in form visible without having to scroll?

- ✓ Did you eliminate extraneous navigation from the page?

- ✓ Are you asking only for the minimum contact info that you need?

- ✓ Is there continuity between your landing page and your web page?

- ✓ Do you have a privacy policy link or statement near the submit button?

- ✓ Is your submit button more interesting than just "Submit"?

- ✓ Is your landing page as focused as your elevator speech?

- ✓ Did you articulate the value of your giveaway item (white paper, discount, etc.)?

- ✓ Did you use trust icons and testimonials where appropriate?

✓ Did you offer multiple contact options (phone, email form, live chat, etc.)?

✓ Did you use light boxes (pop-outs) to offer additional information without the visitor having to leave the page?

✓ Are you using your confirmation page to "remarket" to the visitor? (Follow us, share this page, additional offers, survey, etc).

✓ Is your offer time sensitive to create a sense of urgency?

✓ Are you creating separate landing pages to segment your leads? (PPC, display advertising, email, print)

✓ Have you designed your page as a template so that you can repurpose the page in the future?

✓ If you have a multi-step process, did you make it clear how long it will take or how many steps it will take? (Take our two-question survey, etc).

5

DISPLAY ADVERTISING:
WHAT YOU'RE MISSING

By Darryl Chenoweth

As a digital marketer, it's always interesting to consider the evolution of online behavior and what people are doing while on the web. Outside of communication (email and instant messaging) and some eCommerce, there are three typical online behaviors – search, surf and social. Surfing accounts for the largest percentage of time spent online. Consumers are now spending more than half of their media time surfing popular news, entertainment and lifestyle sites on the Internet. They also spend more time online than watching TV, and reading newspapers and magazines combined! Given these consumer behaviors, it's no surprise Internet marketing dollars continue to shift from traditional offline marketing mediums to an assortment of online marketing channels.

How Display Fits in the Digital Marketing System

Since this chapter considers display advertising as an online marketing strategy, it's important to understand where it fits in the digital marketing world. As illustrated in the simple digital marketing system (Figure 11), display fits into the paid search and surf pillar. Paid search targets people who are ready to buy and searching for products and services online. Display, on the other hand, targets potential consumers in your chosen geographic area who are surfing online. People spend countless hours surfing the web with little or no intention of making a purchase. As they are surfing, they come across display ads, which function much like traditional billboards (except much more effectively). Online display ads are targeted, so they're much better at capturing the attention of searchers who are more likely to convert. Display ads drive targeted traffic to your chosen destination and more accurately fulfill specific marketing objectives because of their contextual nature.

Figure 11: The Digital Marketing System

For any marketing objective to be successful, it must be aligned with a company's brand strategy and business goals. Marketing objectives also need to leverage all aspects of a marketing plan, including meshing offline marketing with online tactics. Display in isolation is primarily an online display or banner advertising solution that builds brand awareness and brand affinity. Even as a standalone strategy, display advertising works exceptionally well. There have been several studies that show advertisers who run PPC along with complimentary creative display ads experience better results than running search engine campaigns alone. In some cases, using search and display advertising together resulted in a double-digit increase in conversion rate. It's rational to assume that if people see your brand while surfing and also when on major search engines, they are more likely to buy from you.

How and Why to Use Display Advertising

The consumer buying funnel can be broken into three different buying phases – awareness of a need, consideration of a purchase and buy immediately. Display advertising is a very cost effective method that targets those in both the awareness and consideration phases. During these phases, consumers have started the process of researching and comparing options, and may even be aware of your brand. There's no better time to ensure your brand remains top-of-mind for individuals looking to fill a buying need but haven't yet made a decision. Display is also an effective method of brand recall and building brand affinity as more consumers will remember you if and when they're in a position to purchase your product or service.

Once you've determined display advertising is an appropriate choice to build your brand strategy and meet marketing and business objectives, you need to set a budget. The most significant factor for developing a budget is targeting. Because display advertising can be targeted towards an audience of your choosing, it's more efficient and cost effective than traditional advertising.

Target Your Ads

There a many ways to target your display campaigns including advanced techniques like geographic targeting, site specific targeting and behavioral targeting. Additionally, remarketing and retargeting are powerful technologies that remember consumers who visited a website or searched for a product and then display relevant ads on other sites they visit. These techniques create top-of-mind awareness for your brand and help bring consumers back to your site.

Geo-targeting is best suited for display campaigns that want to target a specific area. It's important to make sure your ads are targeted to your chosen audience in a given geographic location. These geo-targets can be local or metro, regional or even national depending on what your business is trying to accomplish.

Site specific targeting is the use of top publishers or premium sites as strategic tools. Your ads are displayed on highly recognized sites or a mix of relevant niche sites with good traffic. The result is a cost effective method of gaining maximum visibility and building your brand on popular sites.

Behavioral targeting can provide segregation into a number of targeted areas by displaying your ads to people who have shown recent online behaviors and interests that are relevant to your business.

More common behavioral targeting would display your ads to groupings of sites that feature content related to your business or on category specific sites relevant to your business. For example, if your business is in the home improvement space, ads may be placed on do it yourself home improvement websites. Other examples of behavioral targeting could be in the auto, entertainment, fitness, and food or sports areas. There are numerous targeting possibilities and even overlapping opportunities between different behavioral targets. However, it's important to note that people aren't always going to be more interested in you when only targeting industry related sites. It's a great place to start and get visibility but there are also many great sites to consider with quality traffic. As such, engagement based results should be the primary consideration for optimizing display campaigns. Ensuring ad dollars are directed towards sites that drive the best quality visitors in the most cost effective manner is paramount to a successful campaign.

Demographic targeting is where a target audience is based on demographic factors such as gender and age. If your website collects data on visitors, it's always a good idea to use the information at your disposal to create more demographically targeted ads. Males between the ages of 18-34 are a much different audience than females over 50 years old, so figure out whom you want to reach and then optimize your ads for that specific audience.

For both inexperienced and experienced digital marketers, there are resources that can be utilized for engagement based optimization. A good Internet marketing consultant can set you up on one of these platforms, which will optimize most aspects of your campaign including the availability of an extensive network of websites and ad space inventory that reaches the vast majority of your online audience. The platform technology can automatically and dynamically steer your ad budget to the sites that are most cost effective in bringing quality visitors to your landing pages and website.

Take Advantage of Remarketing and Retargeting

Remarketing is an outstanding technique that targets your ads to valuable prospects that have previously visited your landing page or website. Many consumers visiting your website leave without ever converting to a customer. These are your most valuable prospects as they've shown an interest in your product or service by visiting your site.

For example, a surfer clicks on your campaign ad. When they click on the ad, they come to your landing page or website that has been proxied for tracking purposes. At that point, a tracking cookie is placed on their browser to make sure they can be identified as a visitor to your website. Then, as they surf other sites supported by specific chosen advertising partners, your display ad is carefully and repeatedly shown. The goal is for your brand to stay top-of-mind with interested site visitors and also attempt to bring them back into the buying funnel and hopefully to the purchasing phase.

Retargeting is a technique that can be incorporated as part of a display advertising solution. Retargeting combines two advanced targeting technologies – search and site retargeting – to build top-of-mind awareness with only the most relevant of prospects.

Search retargets prospects by showing your display ads to consumers who have searched for keywords related to your business. Serving your display ads in front of active searchers for your product or services is meant to familiarize your brand and entice them to visit your site.

Site retargets consumers who have previously visited your website and your display ad is shown to them repeatedly as they surf. Much like remarketing, this builds top-of-mind brand awareness and encourages prospects to return to your website, which in turn boosts the results of your online marketing efforts.

Other Important Elements of Display Advertising

Many businesses often jump into display advertising without understanding how and why it can help enhance their digital strategy. Once you do have a firm grasp on display and its function within the digital marketing framework, there are a few more granular areas of display that can really elevate your campaigns to the next level. Paying close attention to these details can help increase your conversions and achieve higher and higher marketing ROI.

Creativity and Design

In addition to targeting considerations, the creative design requirements for your display ads are also extremely important. Approximately 67% of display or banner placements are presented to consumers in one of three ad sizes.

As with most visual marketing strategies, bigger is better, and maximizing available ad space with the biggest ad sizes works best. Leading the way in CTR are the medium rectangle (300 x 250 pixels), wide skyscraper (160 x 600 pixels) and leaderboard ad (728 x 90 pixels) formats and sizes. Your ads can be static or animated.

Regardless of size, design ingenuity will help create powerful, eye-catching, thought provoking banner ads that have strong calls to action and promote both your message and your brand.

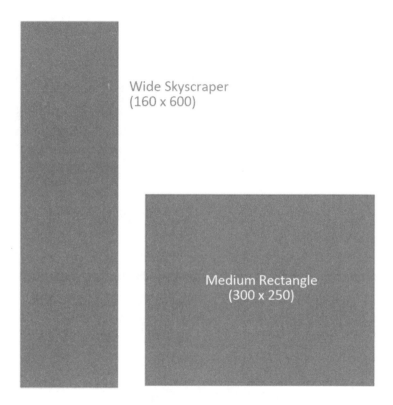

Figure 12 – Display Leaderboard

Figure 13 – Display Skyscraper and Rectangle

Landing Pages

The primary goal of display advertising is to drive clicks back to your landing page or website so you can deliver your key brand messages and convert visitors to take specified actions leading towards a purchase. In many circumstances, you will have implemented a conversion-oriented landing page on which there is no navigation and no escape for visitors other than clicking on your calls to action. Converting, goal-specific landing pages are a great way to guide, direct and funnel visitors towards your desired objectives. They're also an effective method of split testing different pages and details in order to better understand what resonates with your consumer. Many times even the slightest of changes can result in a substantial conversion increase.

Track and Optimize

With every campaign, overall results and driving maximum return on advertising investment is critical. Therefore, it's important to track your campaigns with key metrics and benchmarks. Over time, campaign-tracking reports will provide analytics and results that can be used to further enhance your campaign. Typically 3 – 4 months will enable you to gather enough business intelligence to refine and optimize a display campaign.

Display Campaign Results

You are now armed with the knowledge that display advertising reaches consumers as they surf. The primary goal is to familiarize consumers with your brand and build top-of-mind awareness. It's all about creating a positive impression of your brand and enticing a digital handshake (site visit).

When looking specifically at campaign media spend, impressions and clicks are the key advertising metrics since consumers typically encounter display ads over several months before finally making a purchase. Once consumers have clicked on your ad they'll be taken to your landing page or website. At this point your targeted ads have done their job and your creative design and powerful calls to action take over. Now you want to further enlighten and engage your prospective customer and pull them through your desired conversion funnel.

In the display campaign results example (see Figure 14) you'll find several elements for consideration as key metrics in a display awareness campaign. These results indicate a successful campaign including performance optimization as noted by campaign improvement over time.

Ad Spend Jan-Apr 2013	Impressions Jan-Apr 2013	Re-Marketing Impressions	Landing Page Visits	Web Events	Conversion Rate (Visits to Events)
$70,000	139,885,123	1,921,513	246,563	50,011	20.3%

Ad Spend May 2013	Impressions May 2013	Re-Marketing Impressions	Landing Page Visits	Web Events	Conversion Rate (Visits to Events)
$10,000	21,411,780	187,516	52,450	17,283	33.0%

Figure 14 – Display Campaign Results

Budget. The budget for the month of May ($10K) was much less than the average budget of the previous four months ($17.5K).

Impressions. There were less overall impressions in the month of May (21.5 Mil.) than the monthly average from January to April (35 Mil.), but since the traffic was targeted it likely converted at a higher rate.

Clicks (or landing page visits). Landing page visits in May (52K) were also slightly down from the January-April monthly average (61K), however since the traffic was targeted there was likely an increase in web events and conversion rate.

Web events (clicks on specific calls to action). This is where you can really see the campaign efforts paying dividends. The monthly average number of web events from January-April (12.5K) was actually less than the 17K web events that took place in May (despite a smaller budget and less impressions and clicks to the landing page).

Conversion (on web events/landing page visits). The campaign results underscore that the driving force being display advertising success isn't the amount of traffic or dollars spent, it's conversion. Believe it or not, a targeted display advertising campaign costs less money and delivers better results, which means you save money on marketing and still make more sales!

Why Invest in Display Advertising?

The primary reason for investing in display advertising is to stand out amongst the crowd and expand your advertising reach to the areas consumers are spending the majority of their media time. Here's a list of the main takeaways regarding display advertising:

- Give your PPC campaigns a significant click lift
- Geo-target your ads from local to national
- Retarget consumers who have visited your website
- Track, measure and optimize your results
- Build your brand and boost your marketing ROI with cost effective campaigns

6

SEARCH ENGINE OPTIMIZATION:
IT'S NOT DEAD

By Andre Savoie

Has earning top rankings on Google and other search engines become something you can legitimately do yourself (or in-house) if you're willing to read, study and learn? If not, is it still necessary to hire consultants or marketing firms that have expertise in the techniques used to obtain these top rankings? Or is SEO just simply a thing of the past, and no longer worth pursuing?

The reality is that search marketing is becoming a more significant driver of business and market share expansion than it ever has been in the past. While SEO is not the complete answer (as a company must have a solid PPC strategy as well) if done well, it can provide companies with an outstanding return on investment. Unfortunately, if done poorly, SEO can have a dramatically negative impact on a business (which we'll cover later in this chapter when we discuss Panda and Penguin). SEO consultants and companies are quick to talk about the tricks and techniques they use to help your website magically float up the search rankings, but what they seldom warn you of is how these same techniques are resulting in companies being kicked out of Google's search rankings completely. And that undoing the damage can cost many times more than you paid the search consulting firm in the beginning.

But as with most things, the difference between the "black-hat" techniques that expose companies to the wrath of Google, and the Google endorsed methods (what WSI refers to as *Adaptive SEO*) are not simple to understand on the surface. After all, assuming you even know what Google's Search Quality Guidelines are, or what great content is and how to produce it, if no one visits your website, will it matter? The simple answer is no.

The first question business owners and executives usually ask is "how do I get to the top of Google rankings", followed closely by "how long is this going to take"? The reality is that there are no simple answers to these questions, and definitely no "one size fits all" strategy. Those of us who have done this long enough have seen many cases of the same strategy work quickly for one website and taking longer (or not work at all) for another site to know that each case is unique.

With all this said, it's easy to understand why the vast amount of information floating around might encourage business owners and managers to believe they can manage their online marketing in-house. But the reality is that the competition for the top spaces in search results has never been more crowded, more competitive, and faster changing than it is today.

In fact, with all things being considered, one could make the argument that businesses need outside help now more than ever. Let's find out why, and what you can do about it.

A Brief History of SEO

Ever since people began to take notice of the common factors that were shared among websites that ranked, those in the industry began cobbling together "best practices" or "how to guides" that listed these common factors and explained how mastering them would ensure your site ranks well.

For instance, early on, people began to notice that placing keywords within the certain snippets of code on their websites called "meta tags" seemed to have a positive impact on rankings. Those websites which had lots of good keywords ranked well, and so it became "best practice" to place as many keywords as possible in these areas of the website.

Later on, this became known as "keyword stuffing" and is now frowned upon. However, the cycle which led to the advent of keyword stuffing has been repeated over and over again by those who are supposedly experts in the field. After keyword stuffing came the advent of link farms, after link farms came content farms, and on it goes.

All of this leads us to Rule #1 in SEO.

SEO Rule #1:
You Can't Beat The System

Ever since people began to correlate the impact of minor changes they made on their websites to better rankings, the dangerous notion has taken root that these minor changes must somehow be the magic reason for the improvements, and that more of this magic formula must be a good thing. While this seems like sound logic, the reality is that there are hundreds of factors which determine how websites rank, and Google (or any other search engine) has not publicly disclosed these factors to anyone.

For business owners, this means that you can't crack Google's code, or latch on to one thing that you found on a website that is only open for a limited time, and is so successful that they can't share it with the public. There are no "get rich quick" schemes when it comes to Google rankings, and you can't beat the system. The only way is to do it the hard way.

Enter the Google Animals – Panda and Penguin

As if Google needed to prove the validity of SEO Rule #1, in the last few years they have introduced monumental changes to their ranking algorithms using the names of cute, cuddly animals to somehow soften the blow. The irony is that as cute as a panda or a penguin can be, many website owners were financially devastated by the impact of these changes as they helplessly watched their website rankings plummet in a very short time frame.

You can read everything there is to know about these updates by doing a quick Google search, but for the purposes of this book the most important thing to understand is that the real impact of the Panda and Penguin updates is that they have re-defined what is considered "good quality" work on the web. Google's primary goal has always been to deliver users the "best" websites that match their search query, and Panda and Penguin offer new standards for what qualifies as the best.

The Panda update created a new set of guidelines for what qualifies as "high quality" content. However, for those who are not familiar with it (including many SEO companies who still deliver their services using pre-Panda techniques), it might be easier to list what does not qualify. Specifically, Panda was originally created to reduce the visibility of websites that produced lots of content that was lightly written on a given topic. For instance, they rationed that you could not write a good article on "What to do after a divorce" in 300 words or less, and so they began rooting out these types of sites which created lots of content that wasn't very thorough in favor of more detailed treatments of these topics.

Over the last year or so, Panda has been through several updates and it seems the guidelines continue to get more specific. The end result is that Google has sent a very loud message that they want to see website owners produce in-depth, high quality content that its users will benefit from reading.

The Penguin update dealt with quality guidelines as well, but specifically addressed the area of link building. This whole topic of links deserves its own chapter, but the end result was very similar. Websites that had previously benefitted from obtaining lots of links from low quality sources were negatively impacted. With Penguin, Google set guidelines for what a high quality or "earned" link should look like, something which had never been established before.

The unfortunate thing is that much like trying to define beauty, Google's attempt to define quality has left a lot of room for debate among those who follow such things. The over-arching theme was that websites would be rewarded for producing high quality content and earning legitimate high value links, and the real question then becomes what is high quality content, and how do you find the time to create it or earn a link for this?

The sum of all these changes is that Google wanted to reinforce SEO Rule #1, and to introduce us to SEO Rule #2.

Evolution of Content Based Marketing

After reading all of this, we won't blame you if you wonder what the heck you should be doing if you want to improve your online visibility. Don't feel alone, many other business owners and entrepreneurs are wondering the same thing.

The reality is that the one strategy which never seems to go out of style, no matter how far back you study the Internet, is that if you want Google to reward your site and bring you those throngs of eager visitors, you must create something of value, something people genuinely want to read and might share with others.

This brings us to SEO Rule #2.

SEO Rule #2:
Value-Based Content Marketing Never Goes Out of Style

First let's explore the concept of value based content marketing and define what it is, and what it isn't.

What is Value-Based Marketing?

In a nutshell, most experts simplify the driving force behind the Internet as the search for answers to problems or questions. If someone wants to find out the best way to cut a chicken, they search the Internet for articles, recipes and even videos showing how to prepare, cut and even cook the chicken.

This simple act of searching for answers should be an important concept for business owners to grasp, as the goal of their website should be to create and offer the kind of content that answers the questions of potential customers. Chances are that your core product or service solves a problem in someone's life, and your goal should be to focus on helping people find answers to those problems.

In practical terms, this means taking the time to research who your customers are, and then identifying their problems or concerns. Within the industry we use a fancy word for this called "personas" or profiles of the typical types of customers each business has. By identifying those personas you can then do a better job of creating targeted, value based content that they will want to find and actually read.

Let's take an example of a home building company; some of their customers are new families, some are empty nesters. If they want to appeal to both, they should probably create content that explains how their homes are a good fit for either new families or empty nesters. Is the neighborhood low in crime, does it have good schools, or are there patio homes with small yards that would be easy to maintain? All of these would make good, value-based content for a website.

Now, that doesn't mean you have to give away all your trade secrets for free on the Internet. Ideally, you should give your website visitors enough valuable information so that you can demonstrate your expertise, and offer to fix the problem if they are unable to fix it themselves or are looking for a vendor to do so.

What Value-Based Marketing is NOT

As discussed earlier, when people find a correlation between what they do and website improvements, it usually leads to doing more of it. And when it comes to content marketing, companies have been trying to write lots of website pages designed specifically for search engines that would get rankings for certain phrases. This practice is ultimately what led Google to the Panda update in the first place as websites put up hundreds or thousands of pages that were written for a specific keyword but offered little or no value to the customer. Yet this is precisely the approach many SEO consulting firms are still taking today!

With this in mind, we can safely say that value-based content marketing is NOT writing pages just for search engines, or just to say you are adding new content to your website. The challenge then becomes to define what constitutes valuable content for your business and your customers, and to set about with the goal of creating that type of content.

SEO Rule #3:
Foundational SEO is More
Important Than Ever

Foundational SEO – what WSI refers to as *Adaptive* SEO – addresses to all the little things which create an effective website that is both optimized for search and for users. Let's go into the specifics here:

Full SEO Audit

With all of the changes that have taken place over the last 12 months in the online world, it's a good idea to start with a thorough audit of your website optimization activities. This includes:

- Evaluating the types of content you have on your website and deciding whether you have worthwhile content or if it needs to be improved.
- Checking your website structure for duplicate content, archives, tags and categories which may be hurting your rankings.
- Analyzing your link profile to evaluate whether or not past efforts to gain more links may be holding back your site.

Make Sure Basic SEO Work is Done Correctly

- Your website should have good metadata that is different for each page, and ideally that metadata localized for the locations you serve if you have a local business.
- On page factors such as H1 and H2 tags and a minimum amount of internal linking should be done properly.
- Your address and phone number should be easily visible on each page so website users do not have to go searching for it.

Mobile-Friendly Design

If you have access to a tracking program such as Google Analytics, it's time to look at those numbers to see how your mobile users are doing when they visit your site. If not, the simple test is to pull up your site on a mobile phone and see what the experience is like. Can you find the information you need? What is the load time like? If you are not satisfied with the answers to these questions, it may be time to consider a mobile solution for your site as this does impact search engine optimization.

Evaluate the Components of Your Comprehensive Digital Strategy

It's hard to improve a digital marketing strategy without determining the effectiveness of your current tactics and whether there are gaps and pieces missing.

Personas and special offers. Have you identified the various personas of the typical customers who buy from you, and have you considered creating special offers for each of them?

Service related content and blogging. What types of website content do you have planned for the year? Do you have enough content on your website that covers each of the products or services you offer? If not, consider adding pages as needed, then developing a blogging strategy to provide additional content about those products or services with the goal of adding value and solving problems.

Premium content. In the last year or so, many site owners have turned to creating what we refer to as "premium" content that users might want to download in exchange for an email address, or possibly register for. This type of content usually takes the form of advanced reports, eBooks or even webinars. The type of premium content you produce will be specific to your business, but it can be a valuable addition to your website and very enticing to users who are looking for more detailed information about their problems or concerns.

Social media. Do you have a plan for actively managing your social media presence? This topic requires its own full chapter, but it's important to note that Google and other search engines are now looking at social factors in determining how websites rank. In other words, a website that has good related activity on social media accounts is considered more relevant these days than sites that do not have this type of activity.

Email marketing. While not specifically related to SEO, email marketing is still a viable part of digital marketing. Our suggestion is to incorporate email newsletters as part of your overall content and social strategy for best results. For more information on effective email marketing, skip to Chapter 9.

Google authorship. This one is relatively new, but is something you should probably look into if you haven't done so already. Google now is tying content from websites to a Google+ account, allowing you to connect your content to your profile with the side benefit of having your photo show up in search results. While the early opinions are mixed about the SEO benefits of Google Authorship, there seems to be no downside to claiming your profile and linking your content as a way to improve your search results.

Develop a Linking Strategy

A dedicated link strategy can go a long way in helping your site rank better, increase traffic and generate more social signals. A dedicated link strategy involves the following:

Link clean up. It's a good idea to do a clean sweep of past links that may be holding your site back. Link removal can be tough, but it's worth the time and effort if you have problem links in your profile.

Claim profiles. Claiming local profiles might be the number one single piece of SEO advice we can give, especially for local business owners. Make sure to claim your free business listings on every major local site you can find, starting with the big ones like Google, Bing, Yahoo, Yelp, Merchant Circle and other similar sites. When you do this, it's important to use a consistent set of data when you build those listings so that search engines find the same address, phone number and website address. This consistency across directories can greatly help with local visibility, especially in the local rankings.

Social profiles. Claim and fill out social profiles such as Facebook, LinkedIn and Twitter. While we're not big advocates of claiming hundreds of social profiles just for the sake of doing it, we do recommend claiming the major social profiles so that you can at least claim your spot there, and make sure that the critical data (again phone numbers, website url, etc) are all correct and up to date.

Create great content. Nothing earns links more naturally than great content. Think about any piece of content you've personally shared or linked to – chances are you did so because you found it valuable and believe it will bring value to your social circles. People share content that makes them look smart or funny, even if it's not their own.

Link outreach. Building relationships with other companies and websites that you might potentially develop a partnership with to share content is always a good idea. If you can locate sites that you can contribute content to or exchange information with that usually benefits both parties.

SEO Rule #4:
The Rules Will Change

After everything we've seen over the last year, the one thing you could say about the Internet business is that things will continue to change. Search engines like Google will continue to re-define what constitutes a "good quality" website, mobile users will eventually overtake desktop users making the mobile experience all that more important, and social media users will continue to embrace sites like Facebook and Twitter to share their experiences.

We know that as the online experiences change, so will the demands on business owners to change with them and offer users what they want. If you need proof, just think back to what websites were like just a few years ago, and what life was like pre-Facebook. If the changes in that short time frame are any indication, you can expect much more of the same in the coming years.

7

SOCIAL MEDIA SHAKEDOWN

By Rob Thomas and Tracy Spence

Many businesses want to deny it, but social media is positioning itself at the core of digital marketing. While it might be difficult to keep up with the rapidly shifting social landscape, the businesses that are finding a way to make social work are reaping the benefits.

Despite the plethora of social platforms that seems to grow every few months, there are four main platforms that offer businesses a unique set of opportunities: Facebook, Twitter, LinkedIn and Google+.

Facebook

Using Facebook as a marketing strategy is not a decision most companies take lightly. Many CEOs and business owners are very reluctant to be found on social media at all, but Facebook in particular seems to frighten business people as they see it as a potential risk.

If handled correctly, Facebook can become your marketing partner and is a relatively cost-efficient method for companies to increase brand awareness and consumer engagement.

Although Facebook is free for the general public and businesses alike to use, to ensure that you are getting the best return for your investment, whether that is time, money or both, you should have a plan in place to test and measure in order to benefit from it.

In some cases when a company decides to take the plunge, they find in fact that someone has already beaten them to it.

An example of this can be found with Baileys, a part of the Diageo brand.[3] Baileys is a very popular drink around the world, and fans had already set up pages dedicated to the brand. A marketers dream if handled in the right way, all Diageo had to do was invite everyone from the existing Baileys pages to join the conversation in one centrally managed place. Diageo managed to increase brand awareness and engagement with their audience fairly quickly, and have now introduced the same methodology to their other brands and have a large and growing number of Facebook fans. Diageo not only remarkets to these fans, but also to their friends too, exploiting the viral nature of Facebook.

Your company has a lot to gain from using Facebook:

- Increased traffic to your website
- Increased brand awareness
- Increased trust with your consumers
- Increased opportunity for market research

Increased Traffic to Your Website

Facebook is a place where your company can engage with its consumers and direct them back to your website for more information. These links back to your website act in a similar way to your flyer at your shop, or your business card at an event.

Because you are engaging with people who want to talk to you, these web visitors are more likely to convert and become loyal customers than those gained through other methods.

Increased Brand Awareness

It stands to reason that the more places your brand is seen, the more aware consumers will become of your brand. It is important to bear in mind the persona you want to get across to your consumers.

For example, a solicitor may wish to be seen as professional and knowledgeable, and may direct people to informative articles or blog posts on their website.

A holiday villa owner, however, will want to be seen as warm and friendly, and may want to post images and testimonials onto their Facebook business page.

Your persona may be slightly different for other social networking sites and should be planned well in advance of engaging with your consumers.

Facebook consumers love competitions and freebies, and offering something for a share or a like is a great way to gain loyal followers fast.

Increased Trust With Your Consumers

When using Facebook, it's very important that as a business you clearly state what can and cannot be discussed with your team members in advance. Confidential information should be clearly defined and documented so embarrassments are avoided.

However, the transparent nature of Facebook lends itself to trust and relationship building. Allowing people to post comments ensures a stream of positive reviews. Addressing negative comments – with an apology or an assurance that the issue is being taken care of – is another great way to build trust with your customers. Whether positive or negative, it is essential that comments are monitored and responses are quick.

Increased Opportunity for Market Research

Companies can use Facebook to gather important information about a product or service by asking for opinions. A simple poll can glean much needed information. Asking questions like 'red or blue?' not only gets people engaging with your brand, but also helps you optimize your marketing efforts and potentially save both time and money.

This can be taken a step further by asking your consumers to come up with the ideas themselves. Design competitions are a winner on Facebook in many ways. People love to feel they are a part of the brand, and that their ideas really have been considered. Everyone is a budding entrepreneur!

Paid Advertising

Facebook offers businesses the opportunity to pay for advertising on their site. As a business you can clearly define who sees your adverts and therefore Facebook advertising is an effective way of driving traffic to your Facebook page or website.

Generally it is wise to work with an experienced company who will help you prepare your campaigns, create user friendly landing pages and optimize your Facebook advertising with A/B testing in order to get the very best return on your investment.

Measurement and Metrics

Facebook offers valuable insights for business pages that show how a relatively small number of Facebook likes can make a large impact if Facebook is used properly.

What Do Facebook Metrics Mean?

Total likes is simply the number of people who have liked your business page. The more likes you have, the more chance you have of your message being seen on

Facebook. However, Facebook does not just assume that the number of likes is the most important factor to popularity. When we have discussed "a like for a like" type pages with Facebook - where people like your page for a like back on their own page – they say that they understand that these are popular and so have metrics in place to show the value of these likes. This will clearly show fake likes for what they really are. Do not underestimate the value of an earned like.

People talking about this measures the activity that your consumer initiates. In other words, if someone comments, likes or shares your post or content, answers a poll question, mentions your page or checks in at your place. This figure includes shares using a mobile device. Clearly this is the social engagement measurement, and one that any company should be working towards increasing.

Weekly total reach is the measurement of how many people have posted something about your page. While "likes" are self-explanatory, each of your fans will have a number of friends. The viral nature of Facebook is based around these extensions of a fan-base and so your reach is not limited to your fans alone. The numbers Facebook tracks are based on the first 28 days after a post is created. Your post counts as a reach if it is loaded and appears in their news feed. This is why the "People Talking About This" measurement is important as this will show the difference of it appearing in your feed, or being read.

Facebook also shows the views for each individual post and determines if the view was organic or viral. What is not being measured of course is whether the shares, comments and likes are for positive reviews or negative comments.

How Does a Company Get Started?

Once you have decided to take part you should follow a few basics:

- Decide on your goals and how you will measure them
- Decide on your company persona (friendly, professional, intellectual, knowledgeable)
- Plan your comment strategy (what your team can and cannot say)
- Plan your content strategy (Mother's Day incentives, budget day news etc.)
- Plan your resource (who will answer what, when and how)
- Plan negative reviews (how and who will handle them)

The design elements should follow your brand of course, and Facebook should be an integral part of both your online and offline marketing to make a real impact on your business.

Twitter

People who do not use Twitter often ask, "What is the point - with a limited number of characters, how can you really get your message across?" Each Tweet is only 140 characters including spaces, but this succinctness makes it very easy to read many updates quickly and is why Twitter has become a popular social media platform.

When you update Twitter, it will send a "tweet" to all your followers to let them know what you are up to. This generally means that businesses on Twitter are looking for a large number of followers, but in fact you should really concentrate on obtaining followers who are interested in your business niche to get the greatest benefit from Twitter.

By following people who are likely to be interested in your business, you are more likely to gain the right type of followers. As they follow and begin to engage, your following will grow.

It is important to highlight that a person does not need to use Twitter or follow a company or personality to view tweets and conversations. Unlike Facebook, where you can choose to hide elements, Twitter is public and fully searchable. This in itself is a benefit as it means your shared content can be seen by everyone.

It also means you can easily see what your competition and prospects are doing too.

Twitter can be used to:

- Share photos, videos and news
- Gather product or service intelligence by asking questions
- See what people are saying about your company, brand, products and services
- Demonstrate your industry knowledge
- Collate thoughts and ideas into one space

Share Photos, Videos and News

People are very visual so sharing photos and videos is a great way to engage with your audience. Photos and Videos are often shared and commented on. By sharing news articles and blog posts you can generate links and drive traffic back to your website.

Gather Product or Service Intelligence by Asking Questions

Engage and interact with your Twitter followers by asking them questions. This will not only aid your market research, but will make your followers feel they are valued customers.

See What People Are Saying About Your Company, Brand, Products and Services

Monitor closely what people are saying about your business by running a search on Twitter. This way, even if you do not have an account with Twitter, you can respond accordingly.

Demonstrate Your Industry Knowledge

Informative tweets about your industry are a great way to set you apart from the competition. You can stand out from the crowd as being a leader in your field on Twitter and other social media platforms.

Collate Thoughts and Ideas into One Space

The use of a hash tag makes finding things on Twitter very simple. By encouraging users to use a hash tag (e.g. #wsidigitalminds), you can easily identify the stream of conversations that relate to a specific topic.

Hash tags are great for competitions, where users tweet a hash tagged phrase to be eligible to win a prize.

Hash tags are also useful for seminars and conferences. Twitter acts as an instant news feed for those who cannot attend, and gathers the highlights of the event all in one place, complete with photos, and snapshots of the insights that are being delivered to users all over the world.

The benefits of using Twitter in business include:

- Quick content review
- Increased traffic to your website
- Increased brand awareness
- Ideal source for market research

Quick Content Review

Because tweets are only 140 characters long, they're easy to read, and therefore you get your message across quickly. People scan for the things they will find interesting, so the key to a successful tweet is in the headline.

Increased Traffic to Your Website

If your tweets are informative and useful, and include a link back to your site, then this should drive relevant traffic back to your website. Because the search engines are looking for relevancy, and a low bounce rate on your website (a bounce is when someone lands on your website and leaves immediately), your tweets can also improve your rankings on the search engines.

Increased Brand Awareness

It stands to reason that the more places you are, the more your brand will be seen. If Twitter is used as a marketing tool, and used in a way that encourages people to engage with you, then your brand will become well known on Twitter, and as a result, increase your overall brand awareness online.

Ideal Source for Market Research

Asking questions to your Twitter followers will not only get them engaged with your company, but will start to build the trusted relationship that a business needs to grow online. As a result you can also gain valuable market insights that you would otherwise pay a focus group thousands of dollars to provide.

Twitter Promotions

Advertising on Twitter is a great way to build your following. Typically, a business would use this to build up to a big event or product release or to capitalize on a particular event or sales period in the year. Promoted accounts can be geo-targeted to country level, and in the United States down to state level.

A promoted account appears only for people who would find your news interesting based on the people they currently follow. So, if you sell golf equipment, you are more likely to have your Promoted Account shown to people who follow golf celebrities and golf brands.

Promoted Tweets

Promoted tweets are used to reach users when they are searching on Twitter, putting your tweet in front of the right person at the right time.

Promoted tweets are used to amplify messages to your followers or users who are like your followers and therefore would most likely to be interested in what you have to say or offer.

Promoted tweets are typically used for special offers and deals. They are priced at a cost per engagement basis where you only pay when someone retweets, replies to, clicks or favorites you're promoted tweet. This means that promoted tweets are great for growing brand awareness as the cost for every impression (time your tweet is shown) is free.

Measurement

Analytics are available to all paying advertisers on Twitter and offers some high level information including details on trends, activity and followers. However, there are various tools you can use to gather the same kind of information. One such tool, called HootSuite, details your most popular links, top referrers and more. You can also trace activity generated from Twitter onto your website using Google Analytics.

How Does a Company Get Started?

Once you have decided to take part in Twitter, you should follow a few basics (which are not that different from Facebook):

- Decide on your goals and how you will measure them
- Decide on your company persona (friendly, professional, intellectual, knowledgeable)
- Plan your comment strategy (what your team can and cannot say)
- Plan your content strategy (Mother's Day incentives, budget day news etc.)
- Plan your resource (who will answer what, when and how)
- Plan negative reviews (how and who will handle them)

As always, your design elements should remain consistent with your brand, as you further incorporate Twitter as a vital part in your digital marketing campaigns.

LinkedIn

With over 200 million global users, LinkedIn is rapidly growing and business professionals have a lot to gain if they use it effectively. While LinkedIn is generally seen as a business-to-business (B2B) social technology, it can also be used in some business-to-consumer (B2C) environments too.

LinkedIn gained its reputation as a place where job seekers and recruiters came together to validate CVs online, but in recent years, and since floating on NASDAQ in May 2011, the inward investment has enabled it to develop into a full-blown business social technology.

Some of the Ways Businesses Can Leverage LinkedIn Include:

- Build strong individual employee personal brands and a larger organizational brand
- Have a company profile that reflects the broad range of products & services (brand awareness)
- Increase the brand value of the organization by growing individual staff endorsements & recommendations and then build service/product recommendations too
- Use video embedded in personal or corporate profiles to better demonstrate capabilities, product/ service features and/or case studies, portfolios and testimonials
- Proactively connect with prospective customers who will, over time, better understand your capabilities and reputation so that when they are ready to buy, they contact you
- Regularly post relevant, quality content to a targeted audience
- Leverage the various levels of premium membership to connect with and message in a targeted way, dependent upon your business objectives (e.g. business

research, finding talent/recruitment, sales management etc.)
* Use the analytics data intelligently to identify real opportunities. LinkedIn has lots of useful individual and company metrics right "out of the box" for you to target your efforts

Build Strong Individual Employee Brands

If possible, engage with all key employees to develop a consistent approach to the way your company is portrayed across all profiles. Give them support in how to develop professional personal profiles – look at some of the better ones out there and use those as a model.

Increased Brand Awareness

Build brand awareness and engagement by showcasing your company via professional company pages.

Increased Brand Value

Perhaps the biggest difference between LinkedIn and other social platforms is the way an individual and company can stimulate enhanced online reputation management (ORM). This is done via endorsements (the social signal that you have a skill or area of expertise) and recommendations (the evidence that people have experienced these first hand).

You need processes in place to garner these both as individuals and then to grow the company product/service recommendations as well.

Demonstrate Capabilities

Given the choice of reading text or watching a two-minute video, most people will choose the video, especially on mobile devices. LinkedIn now makes the embedding of video in personal and company profiles a simple one click operation, which can really bring your profiles to life.

Proactively Connect with Prospective Customers

There are a variety of methods to identify "on profile" prospect customers (e.g. via the advanced search function, by joining appropriate groups, and seeking introductions) and provided these approaches are done in a thoughtful way, can reap excellent ROI over time. But as with all social media marketing (SMM), this is more of a marathon than a sprint!

Regularly Post Relevant, Quality Content

When you first approach a prospect to "invite them to join your professional network on LinkedIn", they will check out who you are, what you do, and the potential value of accepting your invitation. Seeing that you post regular, and above all, useful updates on your own profile and company profile will influence their decision. Once they add you, seeing that you continue to post useful content, and the drip of good news stories and case studies (in amongst the industry or market news), will mean that when they need your product or service, it is you they turn to, rather than the competition.

Leverage the Various Levels of Premium Membership

Most people just have the free membership, which is a good place to start, but depending on your business goals (to recruit, increase sales, and enhance brand reputation) there are over 12 different types of premium memberships.

Use the Analytics Data Intelligently to Identify Real Opportunities

Finally, whether it's the "who's viewed your profile" data, the "updates" posted by your connections from your home page, or looking at the "follower" and "page views" insight data from your company pages, LinkedIn's useful metrics are growing every day.

How Does A Company Start?

If you haven't got a personal profile already, create one and go through the process of building up your own online reputation first.

Then you can set up a company profile, which is like a mini-website for you within LinkedIn (with home page, careers (if you have any job vacancies), and service/ product pages too).

The major benefit and difference for you is that, while only 30% of people might believe what you write about yourself on your own website, over 70% are positively influenced by your LinkedIn company pages.

Why? Because as you'll see, as soon as you get customer/client feedback - in the form of recommendations for your products or services - the most prominent images and content on your pages is via those third-party endorsements. And prospects are heavily influenced by the recommendation and referral of others, especially when they can transparently see who they are, what positions they hold, and as a result are able to validate the strength and value of those testimonials.

However, as with all other elements of your online and offline marketing strategy, in order to maximize the benefits, and minimize the time/investment required, it's best to start with the end in mind. When defining your LinkedIn strategy, ensure the following:

- You understand what your goals are and how you will measure them
- Your content and updates reflect your overall brand persona
- Any graphic elements are consistent with your brand's overall look and feel
- To plan your daily and weekly individual and company profile update strategy
- Plan your internal resources so that individuals not only develop their own connections, but also seek to encourage those connections (customer and prospects) to "follow" your company pages (so that if the individuals leave the contacts and reputation

stays with your company)

Google+

It's no wonder that, as Google has the lion's share of the search market, most companies are taking a look at Google+ to find out if it might have some benefit to their business. However, Google's two previous attempts to enter the social media space didn't exactly set the world on fire (Google Buzz and Google Wave), and is why some are being more cautious.

That said, can you afford to ignore something that appears to be growing so fast? (Some commentators say it is the fastest growing social media platform today).

Google launched Google+ differently from previous attempts; not only is it a social media platform, but somewhere to connect via video conferencing. It's also a medium to connect with and easily segment and message individuals and groups, as well as all the usual stuff like sharing photos, videos and links. By converting anyone who has a Gmail account to a Google+ profile, users have been exposed to a wider tantalizing world of social opportunity.

In addition, as businesses seek to reduce costs as well as increase revenue, the Google+ "one control panel" feel also exposes users to Google Apps. With direct "out of the box" integration to their mail, drive storage, calendars, and contacts all accessible from their mobile device. This phenomenal growth isn't likely to slow down any time soon.

As well as potentially competing with the likes of Facebook in the B2C space, Google+ also seems to have its sights firmly set on the B2B space. As soon as LinkedIn decided to remove their "events" feature, Google+ introduced Google+ Events, followed swiftly by Google+ Communities (a feature in direct competition with LinkedIn Groups).

LinkedIn will always have functionality (based on the depth of individual career history and capability validation) that Google+ will complement, rather than compete with. However, with Google+ Local (previously Google Places which also had the Zagat rating system) merging with Google+ business pages, this powerful hub of vital company data and third-party reviews is likely to have a big impact on the way research and purchase decisions are made in the future.

When it comes to business, Google+ can be used to:

Provide an effective overview of your business. One that you can improve your SEO with, by providing direct links back to relevant pages on your website or elsewhere. And when your Google+ Local listing merges with it, you can also provide evidence of your expertise, which will help to influence a prospect's purchase decision.

Connect with your audience using Google+ events and communities. Google+ Events is an interesting feature that allows you to send out personalized invitations to people (whether they are Google+ users or not. It also integrates with Google Calendar if they are Google Apps users, by posting the invitation in their calendar, inviting them to accept or decline the invitation right from there.

If you don't have any events to share, then the Google+ Communities function provides a place where you can invite people to join discussions and grow your influence. And of course, once you are connected to someone (directly or through communities) you can see if they are online, and if they have a video camera attached to their device, even invite them to a video conference using Google Hangouts.

Provide regular, relevant, quality updates. The functionality of Google+ Company Pages are slightly different to individual profiles, and are similar to how Facebook and LinkedIn "company pages" are set up, in that they are separate entities. The company "persona" cannot directly invite people to its circles (the name for connecting on Google+), like individuals can, mainly to prevent new companies just spamming thousands of people with unwanted messages (not such a bad thing!).

To encourage people to connect to your company and place your company in their "circle" you must turn to content. Make sure you are posting regular, relevant, quality content in the form of company updates which are shared publicly (and therefore seen by everyone). Once a user has you in their circles you can drop them into one or more of your circles and message individuals or groups as appropriate, to ensure more relevant, targeted messaging.

Set up and connect with Google authorship for best SEO results. This is the way Google authenticates and will, over time, begin to "trust" you or any author as a quality source of content. Identifying yourself as the author of your content by connecting with your Google+ profile is the easiest way to take advantage of the SEO benefits of Google+ and getting your image to come up against your Google search results listings.

Seek out "on profile" prospects to engage and connect with. As with all social media, success (which leads to a return on investment of your time and effort) only comes if you engage in relevant conversations with an "on profile" targeted audience.

There is more than one way of doing this, for example through both your personal and company profiles. As you cannot "circle" someone until they "circle" you, it is important to build relationships with individuals first through your personal Google+ profile and then introduce your business page's content to them, whenever you think it's appropriate.

Another way to do this is to search for mentions of your company name or related topics (using relevant search terms). You can save searches and then check daily via the left "Explore" option, and respond to mentions appropriately. A simple +1 (the equivalent to a "like") lets the author know you value what they've said but commenting shows even greater appreciation and strengthens that connection still further.

How Does a Company Get Started?

Once you have your own Google+ profile (if you have a Gmail account, you don't need to do anything, you have a Google+ profile you just need to complete it) from there you can set up and administer your Google+ for business pages. From there, it's all about populating your profile with content to further build your brand awareness and expertise.

WSI

8

VIDEO MARKETING:
DON'T BLINK OR YOU'LL MISS IT

By Baltej Gill

What comes to your mind when you hear the date February 14th? Cupid? Hearts? Valentine's Day? All logical thoughts, but this was also a very important date in the digital marketing world. On February 14th 2005, the domain www.youtube.com was activated and the world of video marketing was soon to be born.

April 23, 2005 was the day a video was first uploaded to YouTube. Entitled, *Me At The Zoo*, the video shows YouTube co-founder Jawed Karim at the San Diego Zoo. The video can still be viewed on the site, along with millions of other video footage. How much to be exact? According to YouTube, 48 hours worth of video clips are uploaded every minute, resulting in nearly 8 years of content uploaded every single day.

So as business owners, why is it so important for us to pay attention to YouTube? To answer this question, let's take a look at some quick facts:[4]

- YouTube receives more than 1 billion unique users each month
- Over 4 billion hours of video are watched each month on YouTube
- YouTube is localized in 53 countries and across 61 languages
- YouTube is the second largest search engine next to Google
- In 2011, YouTube had more than 1 Trillion views (around 140 views for every person on Earth)

Those stats are great for YouTube, but what about you, the business owner? How exactly does this help you increase your ROI, or drive traffic to your website and store? Well, videos can be used in multiple ways. They can be used to showcase your products and services, help customers make a buying decision, improve your search engine rankings, and build brand affinity.

In fact, a video makes it 53 times more likely that you'll get a front page Google result. Videos also have a 41% higher click through rate in search results than plain text and consumers are 64-85% more likely to purchase a product or service after watching a video.[5]

Before delving into the details of how you can get your video found in search, or how to ensure it helps improve your conversions, let's start from the beginning and understand the key fundamentals of building videos.

Creating Your First Video

Before you go out there and start blatantly advertising your products and services, telling the world why they should be doing business with you or buying your stuff, here is a fact that might be a little hard for you to digest. People don't like being advertised to. When given the option to fast forward a commercial, they most likely would. So if your video itself is turning into a commercial, chances are people will not want to watch it.

A good example to follow is Tom Dickson, the founder of Blendtec, or as he is more popularly known, the *Will It Blend?* guy.[6] Tom's company makes blenders. Now Tom could have easily created a series of videos on YouTube stating his blender is the best in the world and every home in America should have one in their kitchen. Tom could have gone on to say how he is giving such a great price on his blender that you would have to be insane to turn down the offer. But Tom didn't do that. Neither should you.

Instead, Blendtec created a video series called *Will It Blend?* Where Tom would attempt to blend various unusual items in order to show off the power of his blender. Items included everything from cell phones, golf balls, marbles, an iPad, a six foot garden rake and even a Justin Bieber action figure.

So what was the point of this? Well now Tom has over 500,000 subscribers that tell him what they want him to blend in his next video. The video blending an iPad alone has over 15 million views. He has since been featured on major mainstream media outlets such as The Today Show, The Tonight Show, The History Channel and the Wall Street Journal. Not only are his videos entertaining, they are showing his viewers the power of his blender in a creative manner instead of an in-your-face sales pitch.

Okay, so you might not be in an industry as exciting as Tom's where you can use your product in a unique way to capture millions of views. Does that mean you should throw video out of your marketing strategy? Absolutely not. Not all successful videos are funny or viral. If you are able to answer a viewer's question, that can be a valuable video which helps them make a buying decision. So let's assume you are a real estate agent. You can start creating a series of videos of common questions that you might get asked.

Topics such as:

- How to pick a real estate agent
- What to do before selling your home
- How do I know what my home is worth?
- Do I need a home inspection on every home I consider?
- Should I buy or sell first?

This way, you are creating content that your target audience is seeking information on. You can use the Google Keyword Research Tool (https://adwords.google.com/KeywordTool) and Google Uber Suggest (ubersuggest.org) to determine what questions people are typing into the search engines to help build your video content. Although you are not directly advertising for your services, you are providing valuable information that positions you as a leading expert on that topic. Keep in mind that at the end of the video there is nothing wrong with saying "For more information please contact us at" and include your business name, website, email, phone number or any other way you might want your viewers to follow-up with you.

Let's explore some best practices for creating your first video.

Things to Keep in Mind

Before shooting your video, there are a few guidelines that can help prepare you for a successful campaign. Use the following checklist when preparing for your first video:

Shorter is better. According to a study conducted by Wistia: "The average 30-second video was viewed 85% of the way through, while the average 2-minute video was viewed on average 50% of the way through."[7]

You might be able to sit for hours watching a video about your product or service – but chances are most people will not. So keep your videos short and to the point. Typically, if you are able to get your message across in 30 seconds or less – you will keep the audience engaged for the entire video. If you are creating a "How To" video, or any "Informational" video, those videos are expected to be longer so the 30 second rule will not apply. There are many factors to consider, but aim to keep even these types of videos under 3 minutes.

Throw away your crappy camera. Most cameras these days are high definition and are relatively affordable. But even with a high definition camera, if the user has to strain to hear the audio because of background noise, or if they are leaning in towards their monitor trying to make out what exactly they are looking at because of lighting or because you look pixilated – you need to redo your video. Remember, not all video has to be film quality production with three point lighting, a tripod and a green screen. A simple flip camera will do well with the right lighting, stability and an engaging delivery of the video's message.

Don't forget your call to action. As mentioned earlier, don't forget to leave the last few frames of your video with your call to action – whether you want users to come back to your website or to pick up the phone and call you. You want to make sure this part of your video stays on screen long enough for viewers to actually take action. If you already had the video produced and this segment was too short, you can use the 'Pause' annotation inside YouTube Video Editor which will pause the video at that frame.

Also, don't forget to include your calls to action in the description section of the video. This will allow viewers to easily click on a link and be taken to your landing page or website.

Ask users to subscribe and like your video. Just as the title says, ask users to subscribe and like your videos. The next time you upload a video to your YouTube channel, your subscribers will receive a notification and have a higher potential of seeing your video on the homepage of their screen when they are signed in. This means your videos will get more exposure.

Keep it natural. Not everyone is comfortable in front of a camera. One of the best techniques is to pretend you are actually speaking to a customer. Be natural and informative and you will see results.

Get Your Video Found

Now that your video is produced, it's time to share it with the world. There are a few things you can do to ensure your videos get the most exposure.

Embed video on your website. This is the simplest thing you can do to get video traffic. Leverage the existing traffic already coming to your website and embed your video directly onto your landing pages.

Share via social. If your brand is on any social network such as Facebook, Twitter, Google+, or LinkedIn, share your video link on those profiles. This will immediately bring traffic from your fans and followers.

Email blast. If you have an email database, perhaps your next email newsletter can contain your video. Don't forget to encourage people to share the video as well.

Video ads. You can pay for your videos to appear as sponsored ads in YouTube when people conduct a search. There are several types of Video Ads, and depending on the type of video you have created will help determine what the best ad format for your campaign is. For example, a popular way to advertise is pre-roll ads. This is when viewers are first shown a video ad prior to the video they intended to watch. Usually within the first 5 seconds they are given the option to SKIP AD. So this means if you are investing in pre-rolls, you want to make sure the first 5 seconds of your video is what engages people so they will decide to watch the rest even though they didn't have intentions to and are given an option to skip.

Search engine optimization. We mentioned earlier that a video makes it 53 times more likely that you will get a front page Google result. In fact, videos are one of the quickest ways to get onto page one of Google for your search terms. So how exactly can you increase the probability that your video appears on page one of Google for your search term?

Follow these five steps below:

Filename. Before you upload the video to YouTube, ensure the filename of the video contains your keyword phrase or what the video is actually about. For example if your video is about real estate tips, the filename of your actual video should be RealEstateTips.avi (or any acceptable video format extension)

Meta tags. When you upload a video to YouTube, you are able to give your video a title, Description and Tag to help YouTube understand what your video is about. Ensure you include your keyword phrases in all three sections.

Social bookmarking. Submit your video to social sites such as Digg, Delicious, StumbleUpon, and +1. This will let the search engines know your video is popular and is being shared across multiple platforms.

Syndication. Although we are focusing on YouTube, let's not forget the other video sharing websites out there. Submit your video to Dailymotion, MetaCafe, Revver, Blip.TV, etc. This will again let the search engines know your video is travelling across different video sharing websites which increases the likelihood of your video ranking organically in search.

Video script. This is not a factor that is taken into consideration yet, but soon YouTube will actually be looking at the content inside your video as they translate the dialogue. They will check to see how many times your keyword phrase appears. Where does it appear – at the beginning of the video where it is likely to be perceived as more important? Or at the end of the video which is indicating it may not be as important?

Brand Reputation Management

Another way videos can be leveraged is building video testimonials. Getting customers of your product or service to submit video testimonials will increase your brand reputation and conversions. Video testimonials create more impact than written testimonials as they touch people visually and emotionally and are less likely to be perceived as "fake" by owners or employees of the brand. These videos will build and increase your credibility.

So how exactly do you get your die hard and loyal customers to submit video testimonials? The easiest way is to ask them. It sounds simple but it's the truth and it works. You can also think of other creative ways such as running a contest that involves users submitting a testimonial to enter. Or you can use incentives to encourage participants.

Building video testimonials will also help you rank organically in Google when people search for your company name or your company name + reviews. It is so important for your brand to dominate the top listings of the search engine results page for these search terms, so include video marketing in your online strategy.

Creating a Viral Video

Evolution of Dance, Charlie Bit My Finger, David After The Dentist, Gangnam Style, The Harlem Shake, Sneezing Panda, Dramatic Chipmunk, Dancing Baby, Talking Baby – what do all of these videos have in common? Chances are you heard of at least one of these videos in this list and that's because all of these videos went viral on the Internet.

A viral video is a video where the information or subject matter is shared repeatedly via social media, email, and word of mouth.

Wouldn't it be nice if the marketing video that you have produced for your brand also went viral? Well, before you sit back and start counting the millions of views your video is going to receive overnight, let's take a look at some factors.

A viral video is a viral video. All of the videos in the list above were created and published without the intention of being viral and collecting millions of views.

So although it would be nice to plan and create a viral video, it is not always that straight forward and most agencies will tell you that you can't plan to create a viral video.

Do I need to have a cat in my video? Not all videos need to be funny, have pets, or celebrities in order for it to be viral. What about the tragic story of Amanda Todd, a 15 year old who committed suicide but created a YouTube video prior to telling the story of years of bullying she had experienced? In less than a month that video received over 1.5 million views. Or how about the video to stop Joseph Kony, the leader of the Lord's Resistance Army? In fact, that video became the most viral video in history with over 34,000,000 views on the first date it was uploaded. As of April 1st 2013, the video has been viewed more than 97,000,000 times.

So what can I do? We mentioned earlier you can't plan to create a viral video. Well, that is not 100% entirely true. There are ways you can increase your chances of success. Here are some tips:

In your niche market, try to think of the biggest problem or the most common question and then answer it. The key is to be specific. If you go too broad and start answering questions like 'how to lose weight' or 'how to get more traffic', the probability of your video becoming successful becomes slim. Think more in terms of:

- Reduce belly fat with this 5 minute workout while sitting at your desk
- Cut your Facebook costs by 45% with one click of a button

Don't just rely on one video to go viral. Create as many as you can. The more videos you have in your library, the greater the chance ONE of them might just get picked up and go viral. Some of the most subscribed channels on YouTube had to create hundreds of videos before they even had followers that started paying attention to them.

Measuring Results

Like any of your marketing efforts, it is very important to measure results so you can determine how to improve your campaigns, reduce your costs and increase your ROI. You can use YouTube analytics to determine the performance of your videos and gain a deep understanding of your content, audience and strategies that will further improve your campaigns. These are some key metrics and performance indicators you should pay attention to when looking at these reports:

Views. Total views for the selected data range.

Estimated minutes watched. Estimated total minutes of viewing time of your video(s) from your audience.

Traffic source. How your video is being found.

Demographics and geographic. Who is watching your video and the location from which they are viewing it.

Audience retention. Your videos ability to retain its audience.

Lights...Camera...Action

If you are not investing into video marketing in your digital marketing strategy, there are just so many opportunities you are missing out on. Videos can be used to increase your search engine rankings, improve conversions on your website, reinforce credibility through testimonials, add engagement to your social channels, build your brand affinity and most importantly, provide a useful way for your audience to absorb information about your product, brand or service in the 21st century. Not only are videos relatively simple and cost effective to create but they can also be a lot of fun. So be creative, test different ideas and start engaging your audience through video marketing.

WSI

9

EMAIL MARKETING:

A CONSTANT DRIP

By Cheryl Baldwin

The continual expansion and competitive advantage of any company, regardless of its size or industry, relies solely on two things: lead generation and customer retention. Generating new sales and repeat business from existing customers is the lifeline of all companies. Without new leads entering your sales pipeline and existing customers staying engaged with your brand, your company would simply not be able to grow.

One of the best ways to generate new leads and nurture existing ones is by implementing a carefully planned and engaging email marketing strategy. Email is a tool that nearly everyone uses today, and it continues to grow and be more prevalent among Internet users worldwide.

But email marketing is more than just sending a mass message to the people on your contact list. It is a type of drip marketing technique and is best described as a direct marketing strategy that involves scheduling several promotional and educational messages with specific "call-to-actions" via email. It isn't just an "email blast" – email marketing is a campaign that spans over a period of time.

Building Your Database of Contacts

A core aspect to the success of an email marketing strategy lies in the quality of your contact list. The best way to ensure that you collect quality information is to obtain it with permission directly from the contact. Much like how telemarketing wore out its welcome, so has unsolicited email marketing. This is why permission-based email marketing offers better response rates, increased trust in your company's brand and better deliverability.

Depending on whether you are a B2B or B2C company, you will want to collect different information from your contacts. For example, if your contacts are primarily business owners, you would likely want to have their full name, business title, company name, industry, business address, phone number and email address. If you are a B2C company, then you will likely have their full name, gender, age range, home address, phone number, some of their personal interests and email address.

The more you know about your contacts, the more accurately you can segment your database in order to send targeted emails to them.

5 Ways to Build Your Email Database

Ask for it! Every communication or touch point with your prospects and customers should start and end with a request for an email address. If you are a brick and mortar business, include a ballot box at the cashier's desk where customers can provide their email address to receive updates on your latest promotions or enter in a draw/ contest. Better yet, have your cashiers ask the customer for their email address during the checkout process. You'd be amazed at how many people will give you their email address if they feel it is just part of the overall process. Email has become a very popular form of communication, so asking for someone's email address may be perceived as less invasive than asking for their phone number.

Remind them to subscribe. Remind your customers to subscribe to your newsletter every chance you get. Put a call to action button on your website, include a link at the bottom of your blog posts, mention it on your Facebook and Twitter pages, include it in your email signature and add it to the contact us page. It could take ten different ways for a customer to finally take action and subscribe to your newsletter, so be sure to include a link to subscribe everywhere you can.

Provide an incentive. Your customers won't subscribe to your newsletter just for the sake of subscribing. They receive way too many emails each day to just add another one to their inbox they may not read. Incentives such as receiving exclusive promotions not available to the general public, learning valuable tips and techniques that would help them in their everyday life or business, obtaining a free whitepaper and/or any other members-only perks associated with subscribing to your newsletter could help you get some email addresses you otherwise may not have captured.

Run a contest. A creative way to build your database could be running a contest that would require participants to complete a ballot or form to enter. This could be as simple as running a draw for a free product, service or giveaway package. If the offer is enticing enough, people will want to participate – especially if all they have to do is provide some basic information to enter. Promote your contest on your website, your blog, your social media profile pages, your brick and mortar store, at business networking events and whenever you are in front of prospects and customers.

Forward to a friend. Within each newsletter, you should have a "forward to a friend" link. The link should then drive readers to a landing page with a form requiring them to share their friend's contact details. Be sure to set your form up in a way that allows them to share your newsletter with multiple friends, not just one (approximately 5-10 friends are recommended). You should also include a message box where your reader can include their own personal message to their friends.

Determine Your Customer Segments

The same way a clean and complete database of contacts is the cornerstone to your overall email marketing success, appropriate segmentation of that database is pivotal to the success of each campaign you run. After you strategize your email marketing campaigns (keep in mind you can run multiple campaigns at the same time since the audience for each will be different), you must then determine your customer segments for each campaign.

A customer segment is a group of contacts with similar interests in your products or services, which you have created based on a criteria used to create the list. List segmentation is an easy and effective way to ensure that each message is targeted at the most receptive audiences. If you want to engage your recipients, then be sure to formulate your messages so they speak to each segment.

If you aren't sure where to begin segmenting your database, think of the types of campaigns you are running. This will help you determine your customer segments. If your campaign is to launch a new product or service, then ask yourself the following questions:

- Would this product or service be more appropriate for men, women or both?
- What is the age group of the people who would be interested in this product or service?
- Would location impact whether they would be interested in this product or service?

Let's say for example that your company is a hair salon chain and you are launching nail care services at one of your locations. This service would draw the attention of women likely within all age groups, but particularly between 18-45 years old. Also you will want to communicate to the women located around the salon location in which you are launching this new service. There's your customer segment.

7 Ways to Segment Your List

Demographics. These could include gender, age, ethnicity, education levels, occupation, place of residence, marital status, number of children, income or other socio-economic factors.

Interest-based preferences. If you have conducted any sort of research on your database through surveys, then you know certain subscribers have different interests that could help you identify what type of offers / information related to your product or service would be more likely to engage them.

Prospects that have become clients. When a subscriber becomes a customer, it's time to move them to a different list where they will receive emails that are designed for customers and not prospects.

Open rate/click through rate. Subscribers that open your newsletter or click on a link on a frequent basis are clearly more engaged than those who rarely open your emails or click on your newsletter links.

Product lines purchased. If your company has a vast product line, it might be a good idea to address your subscribers based on the product line they've purchased from and give them information related to that product line.

For example, a consumer that purchases an iPhone would likely be interested in iPhone accessories as well.

Average sale price. Take a look at the past purchases of each subscriber. Those who have spent less than a certain amount should receive different information and be spoken to differently than higher spending customers.

VIP customers. Your VIP customers should be remembered, acknowledged and given special attention. Send them exclusive offers and information the rest of your database may not receive.

Tips for Increasing Email Marketing Conversions

A successful email marketing campaign is defined only by its conversion rates and as marketers and business owners we know you should never be satisfied with the response you initially receive. Below is a list of some key strategies that you can follow to maximize your email responses while increasing your conversion rate and overall performance.

Get relevant or get deleted. Consider your inbox. How many emails do you receive from advertisers that you actually read? Probably, not that many, so what makes you think your customers are any different? The truth is we all receive a high volume of emails everyday and in order to manage our inboxes we move through our messages quickly, looking only for the information we need and want to read and deleting everything else.

So when it comes to increasing email conversions, relevancy of your message to the reader is key. By setting up customer segments (as we discussed earlier) you can ensure that the messages you send are tailored to the demographic and interests of your database. Doing this will make your messages more relevant to your readers and increase the likelihood of them reading it rather than deleting it along with the rest.

Allow your email subscribers to update their subscriber profile. As consumers subscribe to your database you should be collecting some initial demographic and personal interest details from them. This additional information is what you would use to segment your customer database. Overtime however, these details will become outdated (people get older, change locations and pick up new interests) so it is necessary that you allow your subscribers update their profile information every year.

By sending out an email asking your readers to update the information you have for them, you will demonstrate that you respect their time by only wanting to send them relevant information.

Include product recommendations and reviews. If you are properly maintaining your consumer database then you will know what products and services they are interested in receiving information on or have purchased from you in the past. Use this information to include product recommendations certain groups of customers may be interested in. This personalizes the experience for the reader and allows you to get other products (especially overstock items you may need to sell quickly) in front of the consumer that they may not have ever seen otherwise.

Along with the product recommendations you will also want to include customer reviews for the products you are recommending. Oftentimes a third-party validation is what is needed to pique a subscriber's curiosity and push them towards a purchase or activation of service. These reviews will work to substantiate your product, service, and company and coupled with the product recommendations will make a big impact on their decision to buy or not to buy.

Ease your skeptics with a guarantee policy. There are still a number of people out there who are skeptical about products or services being sold via email marketing. For this reason, it is important to offer the customer the security that they have the ability for recourse if they aren't completely satisfied with what they purchased. A worry free money back guarantee is always the optimal offering for potential customers. Simply knowing that they can have their money back if they experience any problems with their purchase (for any reason) will help ease their skeptic minds and prompt them to purchase something they may have been too apprehensive to purchase before.

Everyone loves freebies. Consider rewarding your subscribers from time to time with a free gift to show them you value them as a customer. It doesn't have to be much. Gifts like an interesting eBook, a free software download, or a gift certificate for $10 off their next purchase will draw their attention and create the notion that you have their best interests in mind. Gifts can be rewards for previous purchases, tokens of esteem on a subscriber's birthday, or awarded for other reasons. Whatever the gift or the reason, everyone loves receiving something for free.

Use mobile to boost your email responses. Email helps to boost your response rates to offline campaigns, but did you know that mobile marketing via SMS messages (short message system) can do the same for your email campaigns? Since SMS messages are more immediate and intimate than email, they are opened more quickly than an email is. If you know who on your list is also an avid mobile user and is willing to receive SMS messages from you, consider sending an SMS to alert recipients when an important email has been sent to prompt a higher open rate.

Uncover Business Opportunities by Nurturing Your Database

Email marketing at its core is all about relationship management. Your goal is not only to just capture email addresses for the purpose of building a list. It is also to take that list, nurture it and turn your contacts into future and reoccurring customers for your business. Nurturing by definition means to support, encourage, and develop a relationship or person over a period of time. In the case of email marketing you are looking to connect with the contacts in your database, regardless of their timing to buy and nurture them to a point of sale.

Take a moment to think about how valuable your database could be to your company. For the sake of demonstration let's say your database consists of 50,000 contacts (modest assumption) where each contact is worth $20 (low assumption). That would mean that your database represents a $1 million dollar asset to your company! So how do you take advantage of this additional revenue potential?

Unfortunately most companies don't do anything significant with their consumer database. They simply let any potential for sales die as a result of not maintaining a meaningful relationship with their consumers. However, you do not need to follow the same path. Here are seven key strategies to effectively nurture your email database:

Don't underestimate the potential for revenue. The worst mistake you can make when nurturing your database is to underestimate the potential sales of your contacts. Regardless of how close or how far away they are from making a purchase, you need to see every contact in your database as potential revenue. Some of your contacts may take a little more nurturing than others but at the end of the day the stronger your relationship with your database, the more valuable it becomes to your business.

Create a library of database nurturing content. In order to effectively nurture your database you need to have content to nurture them with. This content can leverage existing materials you have used in other marketing campaigns such as events, whitepapers, articles, or even third-party resources. Since effective database nurturing requires you to maintain active contact with your subscribers you need to build a library of content that you can pull from regularly.

Below are some ideas on types of topics you can build your library of content around:

- Customer testimonials via product rating system,

success stories and case studies
- Multimedia content such as videos and podcasts showcasing your products and services
- Invitations to events such as: exclusive shopping sprees, tradeshows, live seminars, webinars, conferences and speaking engagements
- Past archived and recorded events with email links
- FAQs and customer support channels and guidelines
- Additional methods of following your brand via social media profiles (Twitter, Facebook, YouTube, LinkedIn and Google+)
- Product launches, updates or offers
- Coupons, vouchers or contests
- News about your brand

The shorter the better. People consume content much differently then they have in the past. As consumers we encounter thousands of marketing messages each day so we rarely have the time to print out and read an entire whitepaper, watch a 60-minute webinar or read through a full website page. We have become accustomed to digesting information in smaller chucks and in shorter periods of time. So when you are creating your database nurturing content make sure you keep it short and to the point. Otherwise you run the risk of the reader deleting your email before they get to your call to action.

Match your content to buyer profiles and purchase stages. With database nurturing, connecting with your contacts is vital to keep them from forgetting about you and why they wanted to engage with your brand in the first place. That doesn't mean however that you want to blast sales offers to them on a daily basis. Nurturing is a process of getting these people to know, like, and trust you more.

The most effective way to do this is to organize your content and distribute what is relevant to them based on their interests, demographics, and purchase history (essentially their customer segment). Whatever you send out should be somehow related to what they indicated they were interested in receiving from you as part of subscribing to your mailing list. Again, this is why segmenting your database is so important. Your readers will find content related to their preferences much more valuable than generic content.

In addition, there are types of content that work best based on where a consumer is in the buying cycle (awareness, research, and purchase). For example, thought leadership and best practices work best during the awareness stage; comparisons, reviews, and pricing information appeals during the research stage; and information about the company, support, etc. will work best at the purchase stage.

At the end of the day, relevancy is key and the more relevant your content is to your customers, the stronger the relationship they will build with you and the more likely they will make a purchase (or repeat purchase).

Use your consumers to determine what to send. When someone opts in and becomes part of your mailing list, they do it because they feel you are a leading brand in your industry and therefore an expert in the subject that you're talking about. Use this to your advantage. Try sending out a survey that captures the questions they may have regarding the products and services you provide and then use this information in your blog posts, videos, and follow-up emails. Consumers like to have their questions answered, and if you send the answers right to their inbox without them even asking you'll increase your expert status in their eyes.

Multimedia means multi-conversions. Including multimedia elements like videos, webinars and podcasts in your emails can go a long way where buying resistance is concerned. There is something to be said about actually seeing and hearing the brand as you go through the buying process that makes a consumer trust you more and feel more relaxed and comfortable when purchasing your product or service.

Timing is everything. There is no magical number when it comes to how often you should send emails to effectively nurture your database. What we can tell you is that more than once a week is too much and less than once a month is not enough. So we recommend something in between. One way to determine what your email frequency should be is to have your subscribers determine the pace themselves. When you have them subscribe to your database or update their profile in your system ask them how often they want to receive emails from you (between once a week and twice a month). Just be sure that if you ask them this and they tell you that you segment them accordingly so you don't send them emails once a week if they asked to received them only twice a month.

Integrating Your Email Activities with Other Marketing Channels

Throughout this chapter we have talked about how effective email is at building and strengthening a customer's relationship with your brand. But your consumers don't interact with your brand just via email. They encounter your brand through all the other offline and online marketing tactics you are using as well.

To ensure your consumers have a consistent brand experience with your company it is important that your email marketing campaigns aren't conducted in a silo, apart from the rest of your marketing efforts. People coming to your website or other web properties (social media profiles, blog, and landing pages) through search engine marketing (search engine optimization, pay per click) and even offline tactics should always have the option to subscribe to your email list. This cross promotion is after all how you go about building a strong email database.

WSI

10

RESPONSIVE WEB DESIGN:

THE FUTURE

By Doug Schust

Responsive web design is generating a lot of buzz in the digital marketing space these days, even among the guru web designers. So what's all the excitement about?

Responsive design allows your web content (navigation, images, text, forms, etc) to dynamically respond to the platform or device that is requesting that information. This all happens in the backend automatically as grid elements reconfigure themselves to the optimum size, position and scale for the specific view of the requesting device.

Most websites that integrate responsive design focus on three or four sets of design sizes and devices: smartphone, tablet, laptop (960 grid system), and sometimes the larger screens of desktop computers.

Providing adjustable images across these various sizes presents one of the biggest challenges facing responsive design in terms of total bandwidth involved. There are, however, a few development tricks involving HTML5 and CSS (cascading style sheets) that can be used to load the correct image sizes and design functionality based on the device of the user.

Figure 15 – Responsive Web Design Devices Image

Responsive web design (Figure 15) is vital to most businesses going forward, even for those who have built mobile versions of their website. In their latest release of AdWords, Google identified three key elements: location, time and device. Understanding these changes and the impact they could have on your business will allow you to move quickly ahead of your competition.

Responsive design isn't trivial. It takes a concertive effort and dedication to make it work perfectly. Before diving into responsive development, one must carefully weigh the benefits and drawbacks.

By having common and consistent design for all devices that allows the user to have the best possible experience, responsive design is great for generating consumer engagement and can double or even triple conversion rates for various businesses.

So if you have an existing website you will need to seriously consider making the switch to responsive web design (if you haven't already).

For companies out there that have yet to move into the digital world yet, there is no better time than the present to make the move online.

Benefits of Responsive Web Design

Takes Human Behavior into Account

Day by day, the number of devices, platforms, and browsers that need to work with your site grows. Responsive design represents a fundamental shift in human behaviors. Google just recently came out with statistics that validate the main reason to move to a responsive website. They claim that 67% of all searches start on one device and get finished on a second device. This is key for businesses to understand how we as humans move between devices based on location and time of day.

It's also important to consider usability for menus and sidebars. Unlike traditional sites, which have a single layout, responsive site elements need to resize and reposition themselves across many different screens. When done right, these subtle transformations should go unnoticed by website visitors.

Responsive design can present a challenge for designers and developers, but if you select the right company to implement it for you, you will create an incredible customer experience across all platforms and improve your overall online presence.

Elements of Responsive Web Design

Devices

Many older devices are not yet compatible with advanced HTML5 features. As a result, responsive websites might not load as well or look as good as they do on newer devices. Sites should "gracefully degrade" on older browsers—that is, even if the layout doesn't look as originally intended, important text and images will still be viewable.

New HTML5 features should be seen as additive, and should not break a page for users that don't have the latest, greatest mobile phone or software.

Responsive designs (usually three) will be reviewed by the business owner and all stakeholders. Additional design and development work will be required to make sure the different layouts have a unified look and feel.

Thorough testing will also be needed when approving the final designs.

Design

Responsive design requires rough wireframes and "scaffolding" (interactions between elements) to be generated and approved by business owners before designs are implemented. Creating the designs requires more effort than a non-responsive web design and the design process effort will be multiplied by the number of additional scenarios and devices.

Development

After development starts, minor modifications to the design can become more complicated. Major changes might force a complete redesign so always keep this in the back of your mind. Once again, selecting the right web design company will help to minimize these additional changes and extra design costs.

Upgrades

If you are using an open source platform certain website modules may not be compatible with a responsive layout. You will need to discuss how those additional modules will fit into your overall responsive layout and strategy. It's possible you may need to source other modules to work with a responsive design.

Retina Display

New generations of displays on smartphones and desktop computers use high-density screens. Apple calls their high-density screens "retina" displays, since individual pixels are so small, they can't be seen at normal viewing distance. For comparison, a Retina Display iPad contains more pixels than big screen HDTVs. By packing a lot of pixels onto screens, websites look more like fine printed catalogs than traditional websites, but with the added advantage of interactivity.

So is It Worth It?

In the past few years, we've seen an explosion of tablets and smartphones in different shapes and sizes. Mobile-optimized sites are designed for existing devices, but what about future ones? Due to their adaptive nature, responsive designs are well-suited for the onslaught of new phones and tablets we'll see in the coming years.

Your business needs will determine if responsive design is right for your current site. Responsive designs work best for blogs and corporate websites that provide limited or similar content throughout the website, but it also works for homepages and content-rich sites.

Responsive web design is not only popular, it's required if you want to compete in today's digital world. There are many articles promoting its usefulness and some of those articles make it sound easier than it really is to implement. But if you choose a company that has a track record and can show examples of their previous work, your business is one step closer to having a great, responsive site.

WSI

11

MOBILE MARKETING:
ON THE MOVE

By Eric Cook

Chances are as you're reading this book, your mobile device, whether it be your cell phone or a tablet, is within arm's reach from where you are sitting. It could be in your pocket, your purse, sitting on the desk or maybe you're even using it right now and multi-tasking on a call, checking a quick email message or even reading an electronic version of the book. The fact is these smart little computers (yes, computers, because that's what they are) have worked their way into the very fabric of our lives. As business owners, it's important to understand every new marketing opportunity that can help us engage and interact with our customers in this new form-factor.

Sure, you can still make a telephone call and actually talk to someone, but we more often use these devices for text messages, checking email, browsing the web and connecting via social media. Thanks to readily accessible WiFi connections and 4G/LTE high-speed data availability we're also taking more pictures and video (and sharing it), as well as consuming video while "out and about". Ever hopped on WiFi during a hotel stay and watched a movie on Netflix? Try it next time and save the $14.95 for the in-room movie fee!

When it comes to time spent with all types of major media, eMarketer found that time spent on a mobile device has increased over 270% over the past four years, growing from 22 minutes per day to 82 minutes in 2012. While still not the largest category (watching television maintains the top position with 278 minutes per day), mobile growth rates are astonishingly higher than any of the other categories. Not surprisingly, both radio and print have decreased over the same period (-6% and -31% respectively) with 92 minutes spent listening to radio and 38 minutes (less than mobile) reading print.[8]

As consumer behavior continues to change, we are now in the midst of the "third screen evolution". It all started in the late 1920s with the advent of the television, which was the first platform where marketers' messages could be seen, as well as heard. Here we have the "first screen". Fast forward to the early 90s and along came the World Wide Web. Now computers from all over the world could be connected to one another via the Internet with easy to use, graphical displays called browsers that made it possible for the everyday person to get online – launching the "second screen". And while there were "smartphones" before the iPhone was launched in 2007, Apple's innovative device set the bar for how this "third screen" would change the way consumers communicate with one another (and how businesses can spend their marketing dollars).

As a business becomes interested in marketing more effectively to the increasingly connected consumer, mobile marketing is no longer a strategy that can be ignored. It's simply the "place" to be if you want to get noticed. Remember not too long ago when you just stood in the checkout line, maybe eyeballing the tabloid magazine covers while you spent your time diverting the kids from putting all the candy in their pockets? According to Google, 59% of us now are using this "waiting in line time" to hop on our phones and head online.[9] We are multi-tasking like never before, thanks to the always-on connection to the rest of the world that sits right in the palm of our hand.

Google also found that 48% of us use our phones while eating, most likely to take pictures of what we are eating and send along to friends and our social networks.[10] Pew Internet & American Life Project's Cell Phone Activities 2012 reports that taking photos is the leading activity performed on a mobile device, followed by text messages and accessing the Internet.[11]

We're even using mobile devices while shopping, and maybe you've even done it yourself. You're in a store and see a product you want to buy, but quickly pull out your phone and search to see if you can find it online cheaper, maybe read a review to see if it's worth buying or find an alternate product that is rated higher (or less expensive). If you've done this, you're certainly not alone, as according to Google, 44% of consumers use their smart-phones while shopping.[12]

And as you would expect, there are apps to help with your comparison-shopping efforts, with one of the more innovative ones being Flow, powered by Amazon. Described as "an augmented reality app that lets you discover information about items around you," Flow makes it possible to easily identify tens of millions of products with your smartphone. Once identified, you can touch links on the screen to learn more about a product, find out about related products, read reviews and, of course, make a purchase directly through Amazon.com. You can even share product details with friends via email or social media.

Hopefully the point has been made that consumers are using their mobile devices for more than just phone calls. As a business owner however, how do you leverage this newfound knowledge into an effective marketing strategy? The good news is that you're past the first step and can admit that mobile is here to stay and worthy of your attention. It's the chosen device of the younger generation, in use with 66% of those ages 18-29 and 68% of those living in households earning $75,000 or more owning smart phones.[13] These are the customers of tomorrow and the ones with the income to spend, which make them attractive demographics to bring to your business.

Social

As discussed in Chapter 7 on Social Media, it's evident that we are connecting with each other via networks like Facebook and others from our mobile devices. In fact, a recent study by eMarketer reported that for Facebook specifically, there were 157 million "mobile only" users of their service in Q4 of 2012, compared to 126 million the quarter prior (an increase of almost 25% for the three-month period). Overall, eMarketer also reports that just over 60% of U.S. mobile phone users are accessing social networking sites on their devices (up from 29% in 2010).[14]

When you think about how to leverage mobile in your social strategies, it's important to note that consumers interact differently on a phone vs. a tablet, although many businesses may lump the two devices into the same category. Those interacting with you on a phone will likely be waiting in line or at some other time when they have a quick minute to hop on and check out what's happening. Knowing this, you'd want to ensure that any messages you're creating are quick and easy to digest by keeping updates short or considering the use of images (remember, they say a picture is worth a thousand words) to make engagement easy. You need to make sure that updates are also easy to share and send along to their friends (and their connections) to help spread the word on your behalf.

Conversely, when consumers are on a tablet there's a good chance they are not "out and about" and have a little more time to engage and take in what you've got to say. AIB Research found that a tablet owner is typically accessing social media while either watching TV (33%), right after they wake up (28%), winding down after work (25%) or at bedtime (23%).[15] When interactions like this take place via a tablet device, they can be more feature-rich and engaging, since the visitor is there with a bit more time and under more of a leisurely pace. John Fahrner, CEO and Founder of BumeBox, said it well when he stated, "When users are accessing social experiences on their smartphones, emphasis needs to be on how you're going to let them communicate... [On] the tablet, all the emphasis changes to content publishing."[16]

Text (SMS) Messages

Second only to taking photos, text messaging remains one of the most popular activities performed by users that own a mobile device. Unlike many of the other activities that are mentioned in this chapter, one of the unique elements of a text message (also referred to as SMS, or short message service) is that it can be used with a standard feature phone. You don't need to be able to get to a browser or load an app (like with social media or web browsing) or require a camera (see QR codes below). Sending or receiving text messages can be done on just about any type of phone and is a quick, two-way means of communicating your message.

It's no secret that we are using text messages as a way to communicate, making it an activity consumers are already comfortable with. Pew Research and Marketing Charts reported that U.S. adult Internet users between the ages of 18-24 send the most messages (median = 109.5 messages per day). Even those aged 45-54 are sending 14 messages per day, which is more than one every hour of a typical workday.[17]

Similar in many ways to email marketing, if not done right, text message marketing can be a waste of time and money (and even hurt your brand's efforts). First and foremost, you need to ensure that you're using an "opt-in" permission-based approach to growing your list of mobile numbers. Don't just take all of your customers' mobile phone numbers and upload them into your mobile marketing system, especially since some cell phone plans still charge for incoming text messages (and you don't want to be sending your customers messages that cost them money when they are not expecting it – that won't end well!).

Speaking of mobile marketing systems, you'll want to use some sort of a text message service that aids you with your sending efforts and collecting necessary subscriptions. These services typically charge a setup fee and then an ongoing monthly fee based on features provided and the number of messages you want to send and receive each month. They will also provide you with what's known as a "short code," which you can think of as a shortened phone number that people will use to send you a message and start the interaction process. This short code will also be used with a series of "keywords" that will tell your system what campaign they wish to sign up for and what topics they are interested in.

By allowing your customers to opt-in to your text message program, you get to leverage the conditioned response that we've developed, similar to Pavlov's dog salivating at the sound of a bell in expectation of food. When your phone rings, vibrates or flashes you know there's a message from a friend or someone you've chosen to hear from and you jump at the chance to read it. According to CITA – The Wireless Association, 95% of all text messages received are actually read by the recipient. Compare this with the fact that if you get an open rate north of 20-30% for an email marketing campaign you're doing well and you can quickly see how text message marketing could potentially become one of your favorite tools on your marketing toolbox.[18]

Leads360 published a report entitled *Text Messaging for Better Sales Conversion* and reported that when used correctly in the sales process, text messages can help to increase sales by as much as 112%.[19] The report reinforced the use of a permission-based approach and making sure the recipient can easily opt-out if they wish at any time. Their data suggests that texting in business is very much an earned privilege in the communication process. So what are some of the "right" ways to use text messages as part of the sales and marketing process? During the sales process you can keep your prospects engaged with sending follow-up information on commitments you've made, reminders for upcoming appointments, acknowledgement of receipts or documents and even requests for missing information. Establish the expectation that you'll be communicating with them in this manner and then leverage your chosen system to keep in touch.

Here's another example. Let's say you're the owner of the local coffee shop and you want to be able to send specials to your customers for discounts on drinks and food at certain times of the day. You put a flier up in the shop that says "Text JAVA to 12345 for food and drink specials" (this is just an example, don't really use this code!). In this example 12345 is the short code and JAVA is the keyword. You could also have other keywords for use like MUSIC or BOOKS when your customers want to know about local musicians coming to the shop or book club meetings. You could even tie this to a QR (quick response) code so those with smartphones could just scan the code and opt-in that way.

TIP: As a general rule, when using QR codes, it's always good to provide the "text" way of opting-in for those that are not using a smartphone.

Your text message platform captures this information and keeps the lists organized for you, making it easy for you to send a "blast" message to everyone the next time the local folk singer is coming to the shop (MUSIC), giving you an opportunity to fill up the place (and hopefully sell a lot of coffee in the process). Some refer to this as "business on demand" considering the power that you have with text messages and the fact they are highly likely to be read. They can also target a specific time frame when business may be slow and are easy (and inexpensive) to manage.

Just imagine if your coffee shop typically sees a dip in traffic on Thursday afternoons and you would like to try and generate some additional sales on what is normally a lazy afternoon. Thursday morning you could send a special offer to your JAVA subscribers and say, "Two for one drink special this Thursday 2-4pm. Bring a friend and say you'll treat!" Now people come in (when you're typically slow), they bring a friend and chances are they may also grab something to eat while they are there. These likely would be people that otherwise may not have come to the coffee store that day (so you're not cannibalizing "normal" business) and helping to get people into the store when you want them to show up.

Here are some of the other ways that you could creatively engage and interact with your customers via text messages:

Reminders. Make sure that important deadlines, events and activities are brought to their attention.

Voting. Get feedback from your customers on new product ideas or allow them to select a winner in a contest or similar promotion.

Donations. Make it easy to support charitable causes (the Red Cross has done a great job with this during recent weather-related events).

Alerts. Bring important announcements to your customers' attention like security warnings, emergency store closings, etc.

Business cards. You can provide your personal contact information in a follow-up text message, making it easy for people to add you to their contacts.

Text to win. Create fun contests with trivia or other creative ways to engage and automatically identify random winners.

QR Codes

One of the ways that business can take an offline experience, such as an ad in newspaper or printed brochure, and turn it into an online experience is with the strange looking "quick response" (QR) codes. You may have seen these before (or the Microsoft equivalent, called a "tag"); they are square, two-dimensional checkerboard bar codes (originally developed for the automotive industry, in case you're wondering). Now, however, these QR codes are popping up everywhere as smartphone cameras and apps designed to read these codes are on almost every phone sold today.

Figure 16 – WSIWorld - QRCode

The consumer simply scans the QR code with their phone's camera and the symbol's embedded information is magically transformed into a code that tells the phone what to do next. You can be taken to a mobile-friendly webpage for additional information or to sign up for additional information on an online form. It can provide you with contact information (like a digital business card) or even launch a video to play on your phone and provide you with an interactive presentation from what would have been a static, printed advertisement. They can even be set to launch many of the common text message functions mentioned previously. The important part is marketers now have the ability to take what once was a static, fixed amount of information and turn it into a virtually limitless method of providing detail directly from a mobile device.

As camera technology becomes even more sophisticated, like what we're seeing with apps like Google Goggles and Flow by Amazon.com, the jury is still out on whether QR codes will be needed down the road as these apps are smart enough to recognize products and even locations without the need for the QR code itself. But at least for now, QR codes seem to be a popular way to get even more information in the hands of your customers while they're on their mobile device.

Location (GPS) and Check-Ins

One of the nifty features that today's smartphones offer is GPS location, which comes in handy when you're using Google Maps to help get you where you need to go. There are apps like Glympse that can even share your location with others so they can see when you're "on your way" – something your spouse may appreciate if you're running late for dinner and you need to prove that you're stuck in traffic!

As a marketer, knowing the location of your customers is also a valuable tidbit of information to have, as you may be able to present them with an offer at the right time, like when they are physically present at your establishment. Or, maybe you'd want to send a special offer to someone that's at a competitor right down the street and you want to get him or her to change his or her mind and purchase from you instead. Whatever the case, mobile users are using apps like Foursquare, Facebook, Google and Twitter to share not only their thoughts and stories, but also their location with friends and those they are connected to.

One example of how American Express is using this to their advantage is through their partnership with Foursquare. As one of the more popular "check-in" apps available today, Foursquare has figured out how to turn checking-in into something fun and interactive. Users can collect "badges" for different categories (like coffee shops, Mexican restaurants, travel, etc), plus you can leave tips for others to check-in and if you happen to visit (and check-in) more than anyone else, Foursquare rewards you by appointing you as the Mayor. Do you know who the Mayor of your business is?

Getting back to American Express: they formed a national deal with Foursquare to offer cardholders discounts when they checked in on their mobile phones at certain shops and restaurants. These discounts are in addition to the awards and merit badges mentioned earlier, and these money-saving offers are designed to reward American Express users (and even change behavior).

Here's a real world example of this strategy impacting consumer behavior. Let's say you're on vacation in San Diego, USA and visit a quaint downtown restaurant for breakfast. You proceed to check-in via Foursquare to see if there were any "deals" available, and since you're on vacation, to show your friends that you're having breakfast in sunny San Diego. It's a Sunday, so the standard coupon offered for the check-in is invalid (only good on weekdays), but there's a secondary offer presented by American Express. By registering your American Express card and using it to pay the bill, it entitles you to a 15% discount off your bill. While your normal "go-to" card is a Visa®, that day you're likely going to use the AMEX card for the purchase (and again when faced with other opportunities to save money). Thanks to Foursquare and American Express knowing where you were (and what you were doing) they very likely changed your purchase behavior.

The other component of the "check-in" strategy is to leverage the customers' interaction with your brand and promote the experience to their network and friends. Maybe you share your breakfast experience with friends (if it was good enough), offering up some much-valued word-of-mouth advertising. Maybe you also leave a "tip" for others that would visit in the future, encouraging them to register their American Express cards so they too could get a discount. Thanks to the mobile device, you helped market both the restaurant and American Express – all for 15% off your bill. Now that's cheap advertising!

Don't Forget Your Website

Avinash Kaushik, author of *Web Analytics 2.0* and *Web Analytics: An Hour A Day*, and Digital Marketing Evangelist at Google, says "never let social media write checks that your website can't cash."[20] Modified for the purposes of this chapter, this could be said as "never let your mobile marketing strategy write checks that your website can't cash."

This means if you plan on engaging your customers with any of the aforementioned mobile marketing strategies, ultimately the goal is to get them to "do something" that will lead to a conversion (most likely, on your website). That may be an actual sale of a product, signing up for your newsletter, requesting an appointment, etc. But if you take the mobile customer to a non-mobile-friendly website, you now are requiring them to do things like pinch, zoom, tilt and all sorts of other finger acrobatics to complete the process. If it's too difficult, chances are all the work you've done up to that point will be lost and they'll quickly click the back button and be gone.

If you jumped to this chapter because mobile marketing was top of your "to do" list that's fine. If that's the case, you may want to backup and read Chapter 10 on Responsive Web Design (or re-read it again now that you've learned that a mobile strategy cannot exist in a vacuum). The concepts of mobile-friendly web construction and responsive web design (RWD) are ones that further support the "check cashing" concept of a well-organized mobile strategy. It also will help to ensure that your customers are experiencing your brand consistently on their mobile device, no matter how they decide to engage with you.

There are many other ways to leverage the mobile device when it comes to marketing your business. We've only scratched the surface here, but hopefully you've come away with the realization that the potential of marketing your business via a mobile strategy is limited only by your imagination.

WSI

12

DON'T FORGET ABOUT
MEASUREMENT

By Miko Kershberg

By this point in the book, you have learned great things that you can (and should) adopt for your business and your digital marketing initiatives.

As has been discussed within many of the chapters, the key to these strategies is measuring and managing the results of your campaigns! So please, enter the world of web analytics.

The Web Analytics Association defines web analytics as the "the measurement, collection, analysis and reporting of Internet data for purposes of understanding and optimizing web usage."

A more recent definition – one that takes into account that analytics is more than just your website nowadays - states that it is the "process of obtaining an optimal and realistic decision based on existing data" and the "study of online experience in order to improve it." These definitions seem more meaningful and relevant to digital marketing.

Measure is What Businesses Do

Every company checks its financial books to see how it is doing. Although businesses tend to have a general perception of things, they always want to verify their financial reports down to the exact cent. In reality, not analyzing your digital marketing data is very much like not looking at your financial reports. You simply can't neglect the data – it could be costing you money.

For the most part, web analytics data is collected automatically (given a simple setup) and you don't need to have a bookkeeper enter the information for us to see the results. Therefore, a lack of data certainly isn't the problem. Quite the opposite – we are living in a world where we often hear phrases like "so much data, where do I start?"

The problem could actually be how to synthesize the enormous amount of data you get from your analytics tools – much more than could ever be used by any human being – and choosing the data that is most relevant.

Just like in financial books, in order to analyze correctly and drive the right recommendations for your marketing efforts, you need to make sure that the data you're collecting has the following three attributes:

Proper Quality

No analytics tool is perfect. Analytics practitioners take it as a given fact that the different vendors are always trying to find better ways to measure and analyze. Thus, the attribute of "quality" should not be mistaken for "perfect", but within the scope of whatever tools you are using to measure, you need to make sure that you're getting high-quality data.

Accuracy

The default settings of analytics tools are generic. They do a great job in representing the basic types and ways of tracking and presenting data. However, the world of digital marketing is changing very fast and sometimes what you are doing online is not yet supported generically in analytics software. Remember that your website and your data are specific and therefore should sometimes require some tweaks in the tool to make sure you're mining accurate data.

Relevancy

Analytics should inform and be informed by business goals. Any data you search for should remain in context. It has to be relevant to you, your company, your website, and your digital marketing activities.

You can rely on our analytics tools and some help from professionals to ensure that your data is of proper quality and accuracy, but the toughest part is to make it relevant.

Measurement Starts at the Beginning

Just as it is in this book, the measurement part traditionally comes last. It's the one common element that ties everything together and shows you how you're doing.

However, in order to analyze, measure and compare, you need a baseline. Your business needs to decide upfront what that baseline is by determining what you're going to measure and how that will dictate whether you're improving or actually wasting marketing dollars on things that are not yielding a good return on investment.

Thus, diving into the enormous amount of data and reporting you get out of the box from an analytics tool without setting the proper foundation is the wrong approach. A better one would be to construct a process and a model that helps you set the path for where you want to head and be able to answer an important question: are you improving or not?

Don't get discouraged just yet, as such a tool exists.

Web analytics evangelist Avinash Kaushik (who was just talked about in Chapter 11), has presented and promoted the Digital Marketing Measurement Model (DMMM) that will be expanded upon in this chapter.[21]

All websites have a purpose. Tracking the basic metrics such as visitors, traffic sources, and page views is potentially important, but it isn't enough data for commercial businesses. These metrics don't really give you impactful data. Impactful data is informed by business goals and must be tailored directly to your business.

The Digital Marketing Measurement Model

The DMMM is a top-down model. Every layer is built on its predecessor with a direct connection that ensures all layers, from top to bottom, have the business context you need and helps focus on the things that really have an impact on your business and marketing initiatives.

Business Objectives

Any web site can be categorized in one or more of the following four types:

Commerce. In this environment, the goal is to get customers to buy directly online.

Lead generation. In this model, the goal of the site is to get visitors to submit their contact information so that you can nurture these visitors into customers.

Content. Content sites revolve around the advertising business model. Example of such sites includes Wikipedia.org. The goal is to get visitors to keep coming back to consume content.

Support/self service. The support or the self service model revolves around providing customers with the ability to find the answers they need regarding their products. This model revolves around the cost savings associated with deflection of call center volumes.

Once you are clear on the type of website you have, you are on your way to identifying your business objectives.

Make sure to seek business objectives that are achievable and easily understood by everyone that reads them. Anything that does not carry those attributes should be discarded from the list.

Goals

Once you have established your list of objectives, you are looking to set goals to meet those business objectives. The aim is to identify one or two goals per business objective.

Goals are specific strategies or even tactics that you will carry out in order to accomplish your objectives. Since the objectives are strategic and high level, you need to narrow them down to specific things that need to be done in order to realize the objectives.

When considering your goals, keep in mind the three key facets of analytics:

Acquisition. Anything that has to do with getting traffic to your website. Make sure to take into account your priorities and to cover – where relevant – all types of sources, whether they're earned (e.g. social media), owned (SEO) or paid (PPC, display advertising).

Behavior. What is the behavior you are expecting when people arrive to your website? Think in terms of returning to your website, time spent on the site, pages being consumed, or videos that should be played.

Outcomes. What outcomes signify value delivered to the business bottom line? Think of those things that you will want your visitors to do that have meaning to your business. Things like filling in an inquiry form, downloading a file, or signing up to your newsletter.

Key Performance Indicators (KPIs)

This step is taking your goals to a more measurable level. Since this is where the data starts to come in, this might also be the step where the involvement of a data analyst is an advantage.

A KPI is defined as a measure that determines how your campaigns are doing in terms of your objectives and goals. A KPI will explain which metric is going to be used to measure the goal it belongs to and will act as a benchmark for you.

Good KPIs must be:

Relevant. This one is obvious. Just because others are using a certain metric as a measurement does not mean it is relevant to your business and website.

Timely. It must be a metric that can be pulled out of your data quickly and with no effort. You cannot be waiting around for data.

Uncomplicated. A KPI should be very simple and straightforward.

Instantly useful. You want your KPI to easily indicate what areas and campaigns need attention.

Here are some ideas for potential KPIs:

- Conversion Rate – the ratio of number of conversions divided by the number of visits
- Days/Visits to Purchase – how many days or how many visits it takes a visitor to buy on our website
- Loyalty – the number of times a visitor returns to your site
- Time – how long does it take to a visitor to return to your site

Segments

One of the biggest risks when looking at data is the aggregates. The other one is the averages.

Typically, your analytics tool will show aggregates of data being collected. For some metrics, you get aggregated averages (such as "average time on site"). However, there is no such thing as an 'average visitor'.

So, on one hand you want sufficient population size in order to make decisions and to avoid a specific occurrence (a visit, a visitor), but on the other hand you need to understand that aggregated data is misleading. Visitors behave differently depending on the medium or campaign they came from, their location, or the day of the week.

In order to solve this, you need to segment the data. If you divide the streams of data into different groups, you can better understand the data and take quicker action.

So, in this step of the model you are seeking an answer to the question: What are the most important segments to focus on for each KPI that will help you understand your goals and meet your objectives?

Here are some straightforward segments to consider (remember to use those that are important and relevant to you):

- New vs. Returning Visitors
- Traffic Sources: differentiate between search, direct and referral traffic. Depending on your specific situation, you can further drill down to paid search vs. organic search
- Originating Country
- Subscribers vs. Non-Subscribers

Targets

Now you need an answer to the most important question: "What does success look like?" To do this, you need numerical values that will serve as indicators of success (or failure).

Remember, looking at data can be misleading. Is 500 downloads of a certain white paper per month good or bad? 1000? 5000? The answer depends on your goals, objectives and targets. For some campaigns, these numbers will be really good, and for others, they'll indicate poor results.

From the other side of things, targets will help you plan your initiatives. If there is a target to get X number of visits per month, the type, nature and budget of the campaign you will be running will be different if this number was Y.

Congratulations, now your model is done. Whether you use a spread sheet, a presentation, a document or a piece of paper it does not really matter. As long as you can see how everything is relevant to your business today and every step is connected to its predecessor, you can be sure that you have completed the first step in your road to improving your digital marketing strategy.

What's Next?

Now that you have your DMMM, what should you do next?

Make it a point to visit the model every few months (or when it makes sense) and adapt it. Typically, from the KPIs down you will need to adapt the model, replace KPIs with new ones, add a segment that has become important and set new targets to new initiatives.

To start, make sure you are collecting the data you need to find the answers to the questions your model is raising. It will probably involve "out of the box" data that you aren't getting from your analytics tool as is and a portion that will require you to do some configurations of your own. A good example for that would be the need to tag your non-Google AdWords campaigns such as email and display advertising. You can find multiple resources online on how to do almost anything that you need or you can always have an analytics professional help you if you're feeling overwhelmed.

Once data is in place, spend time creating your reports and automate them. Analytics tools such as Google Analytics provide great possibilities for setting up dashboards and you can (and should) create one or more dashboards that will represent the KPIs that you set in your measurement model.

Google Analytics also has a list of third-party tools that can connect data and present it in other formats like Microsoft Excel and PowerPoint. This makes your dashboards much more interesting and presentable, but the biggest advantage is that you will be able to present your targets and show how you are doing compared to those targets. This makes reporting much easier for everyone and ads the value reporting deserves.

The last part pertains to automation. Web analytics tools are constantly adding great automation abilities. You can now get your reports delivered to your inbox at various time intervals, but you can also set alerts to get immediate notifications when a KPI drops lower than a given threshold. This enables you to be aware of things as they happen and to identify the cause and take action.

The DMMM Beyond Digital

Take another look at the DMMM and you can recognize that this model is actually not restricted to the realm of digital marketing or marketing in general. This is a great model for any business to realize and recognize its goals, targets and measurement factors.

This is exactly the essence of analyzing data – understanding what to track and the impact it might have or is having on your company, whether it involves strictly digital marketing data or your business in general.

Measurement Beyond Online Marketing

In today's digital world, the line that separates traditional marketing and digital marketing is fading away. Studies support what we all know from our own behavior as consumers, that our engagement with businesses is no longer reserved to our exposure to spots on the TV or newspaper ads or even banners on our favorite news portals online. The path of the consumer crosses this artificial line of offline and digital.

The challenges of measuring marketing are broader than just the website (even broader than all of your web properties and strategies such as social, mobile, and email). Business owners and marketers should find a way to set goals, track and measure holistic marketing initiatives and strategically build campaigns that yield results.

For example, let's say you're a business that only sells items at your brick and mortar location. Your website and all of your digital marketing tactics should be driving people to your store. The correlation between your marketing mix – online and offline – and the bottom line is where the challenges reside.

Never Stop Measuring

Remember that "if you cannot measure it you cannot improve it." Digital marketing measurement is all about improving what is most important.

Make it your point to focus on the critical factors that make the difference to you and your company, track them, analyze them and concentrate on improving those aspects. Everything else will fall into place.

PUTTING IT ALL TOGETHER

Now that you've reached the end, you're probably a little overwhelmed with the all-encompassing nature of digital marketing. And that's understandable. Digital marketing comes with a steep learning curve that changes almost as fast as you can learn it, which means there's never a shortage of new knowledge. To truly keep updated to the world of digital marketing, you'd need to dedicate at least an hour of your day to read and understand the changes in the industry. And then applying it to your business would require even more time.

For many business owners, there aren't enough hours in a day, and that's where a WSI Consultant can make a world of difference. Working with a consultant frees you up to take care of your business and not worry about the ins and outs of digital marketing. Plus, if you take on the task yourself, you may end up spending more money than you need to on less than optimal strategies. It never hurts to seek a little bit of help when you're in doubt.

If you decide you want to try out digital marketing on your own, that's fine too, but it will take time and energy. If you're going it alone, the most important lesson you can learn from this book is that everything is specific to your business. In other words, the answer to many of the questions you'll initially have is "it depends."

Should you use all 12 strategies outlined in this book? It depends on your business's goals and budget; if the resources are there, you should experiment with as many strategies as you can.

Is social media a good fit for your business? It depends; maybe not, but if nobody in your industry is making social work and you can find a way to leverage it effectively, you stand to gain a huge edge over your competitors.

No two digital marketing strategies are the same, so this book is more of an introduction to all of the strategies that could be potentially helpful to your business rather than a step-by-step manual. This book cannot tell you which strategies will work best for you. That's up to you or the consultant you work with. But rest assured, there is a mix of digital marketing tactics out there for you and your business. It just entirely depends on your goals, target audience, budget, market, resources and a whole host of other details very specific to your business.

NOTES

1. Steven Wise. Http://cdn.oreillystatic.com/en/as-sets/1/event/58/Understanding%20Local%20Mobile%20Consumer%20Behavior%20Presenta-tion%201.pdf
2. Steven Wise. http://cdn.oreillystatic.com/en/assets/1/event/58/Understanding%20Local%20Mobile%20Consumer%20Behavior%20Presentation%201.pdf
3. http://ads.ak.facebook.com/ads/FacebookAds/Dia-geo_CaseStudy_EN.pdf
4. www.youtube.com
5. www.bigcommerce.com
6. www.youtube.com/Blendtec
7. http://wistia.com
8. Chart: *Average Time Spent per Day with Major Media by US Adults, 2009-2012*. eMarketer, October 2012
9. Google Study, April 2011
10. Google Study, April 2011

11. Pew Research Center's Internet & American Life Project, Summer Tracking Survey, August 7-September 6, 2012. N=2,581 cell phone owning adults ages 18 and older. http://pewinternet.org/Reports/2012/Cell-Activities.aspx

12. Google Study, April 2011

13. Pew Research Center's Internet & American Life Project, Summer Tracking Survey, August 7-September 6, 2012. N=3,014 adults ages 18 and older. http://pewinternet.org/Reports/2012/Smartphone-Update-Sept-2012.aspx

14. eMarketer, *Social Media Marketing on Mobile Devices*. http://www.emarketer.com/Webinar/Social-Media-Marketing-on-Mobile-Devices/4000063

15. Interactive Advertising Bureau Mobile Marketing Center of Excellence, "Mobile's Role in a Consumer's Media Day: Smartphones and Tablets Enable Seamless Digital Lives"

16. John Fahrner in eMarketer's *Social Media Marketing on Mobile Devices*. http://www.emarketer.com/Webinar/Social-Media-Marketing-on-Mobile-Devices/4000063

17. http://pewinternet.org/Reports/2012/Cell-Activities/Main-Findings.aspx

18. http://www.ctia.org/media/press/body.cfm/prid/1696

19. Leads360, Sales Optimization Study: *Text Messaging for Better Sales Conversion.*

20. Avinash Kaushik

21. Avinash Kaushik, http://www.kaushik.net/avinash/digital-marketing-and-measurement-model/

ABOUT THE AUTHORS

Husam Jandal

 Husam is a well-recognized International speaker, Digital Marketing Consultant with WSI (8 years), Professor of eCommerce, and Certified Marketing Professional by Google, Yahoo, and he is also a member of the Search Engine Marketing Professionals Organization, member of the Web Analytics Association, and member of the Usability Professionals Association.

Husam is actively helping organizations worldwide to be successful online by implementing the most effective digital marketing and social media strategies, building their online digital assets, increasing their online visibility and brand efficacy, managing their reputation online, and maximizing ROI from the Internet.

Francois Muscat

Francois Muscat is the WSI Area Representative for South Africa. He represents South African Consultants with excellence as he strives to ensure they achieve the utmost success. Francois has been a WSI Consultant since 2004.

Francois has won seven WSI awards including – Best Product Showcase, Excellence in Search Engine Optimization, Excellence in PPC, and two mentorship awards. Most recently he won the National Sales Award as Africa's Franchisee of the Year at Stansted 2009. He also enjoys mentoring many WSI Internet Consultants internationally.

Francois operates his business out of Johannesburg, South Africa and specializes in content, social media and search engine marketing.

Benjamin Smith

Benjamin Smith has 11 years of experience in the digital industry as a WSI Digital Marketing Consultant. He serves small, medium, and large businesses from his office near Milwaukee, WI, USA. He is also the WSI Area Representative for

Wisconsin, Minnesota, North Dakota, South Dakota, and Iowa, USA.

Benjamin specializes in the management of pay-per-click and display advertising. He manages multi-million dollar annual pay-per-click and display campaigns for clients all over the world. He is certified by Acquisio and is a member of the Search Engine Marketing Professionals Organization.

Chuck Bankoff

Chuck Bankoff is an International speaker, author and trainer to Internet Consultants in over 8 countries.

With degrees in graphic design, digital electronics and an MBA from Keller Graduate School of Management, his areas of expertise are search engine marketing, social media management, website design, landing page design and conversion technologies.

Chuck holds a variety of digital certifications including Google Adwords, SEMPO and eCommerce from USC Marshal School of Business. Chuck is based in Orange County, California, USA where he has been practicing Internet marketing since 1999.

Darryl Chenoweth

Darryl is an award winning WSI Digital Marketing Consultant operating out of Ancaster, Ontario, Canada. With a focus on the retail and consumer package goods verticals, Darryl helps clients develop and implement Internet marketing strategies to connect with their customers through a full suite of solutions. Clients are typically senior leaders in business and marketing strategy looking to leverage Darryl's expertise in web development, paid search and display, search engine optimization, email marketing and social technologies.

Darryl has 30 years of direct retail experience including 15 years as a senior retail operations and marketing executive for large retail companies. Darryl is uniquely positioned as a digital marketing expert and a sought-after retail consultant helping businesses transition from offline to online marketing.

Andre Savoie

Andre Savoie is a search and social marketing specialist who has earned certification through WSI's Advanced Internet Marketing Program as well as the Search Engine Academy (taught by John Alexander and Robin Nobles).

He works with clients in the areas of marketing strategy, search engine optimization, pay-per-click marketing and social media technology, such as blogging.

Tracy Spence

Tracy Spence has been a WSI Consultant since 2005 and works with a small but knowledgeable team from her offices in Northampton, UK.

Tracy's digital marketing career has enabled her to build a great relationship with Facebook, working with them on a one-to-one basis to understand their platform extensively and develop her knowledge on how to get the very best out of the platform for business. Tracy has also delved deeply into Twitter and how to benefit from it as a marketing tool, successfully working with many clients.

Tracy speaks at conferences and events around the world about social media and digital marketing.

Rob Thomas

Rob Thomas lives and breathes social technology and digital marketing.

A WSI consultant since 2006, near Bristol in the UK, he's recognized as an expert in reputation management and business social media. Rob is a professional speaker in the US and across Europe and provides coaching and implementation services to business owners, leaders and their teams.

He's helped clients maximize LinkedIn for lead generation since 2006 and Google+ for Business since its launch in 2011.

Baltej Gill

Baltej Gill is a search engine, social media and mobile marketing specialist at WSI as well as Vice President of M3 Social Mindz, one of the world's leading Internet marketing companies.

Graduating from a technical background in computer science, Baltej has over six years experience in training and educating marketers and organizations on how to leverage Internet marketing in their business.

He has held many Internet marketing workshops internationally and trained Digital Marketing Consultants on subjects such as search engine optimization, conversion architecture, social media, mobile marketing and web analytics.

Cheryl Baldwin

As Director of Marketing Communications, Cheryl manages the ongoing development of marketing strategies, programs and collateral for the WSI Consultant network. In addition, she is also responsible for WSI's corporate communications, social channels and coordinating

various partner alliances. Overall, Cheryl's focus is on ensuring that WSI builds a strong and consistent brand as a top digital marketing company.

Cheryl joined WSI in 2003 and has become an instrumental member of the WSI Corporate team. Prior to becoming the Director of Marketing Communications, Cheryl managed WSI's eStore and the Product Marketing team.

Doug Schust

Prior to his current position as President of WSI, Doug was the longest standing and highest revenue producing WSI Consultant. Having been a WSI franchisee since 1995, Doug has more than 16 years of experience in the Internet marketing industry and over 30 years of total marketing experience.

As a driving force for the WSI brand and a leading authority within the industry, Doug has an intimate understanding of both the challenges and, most importantly, the tremendous opportunity that exists in the digital space for businesses all around the world.

Eric Cook

Eric Cook, a former community bank executive of 15 years, now considers himself a "digital strategist" and works with clients to help them better understand and leverage the power of the Internet as a strategic business tool. An award-wining web designer with WSI, Cook is also a sought-after, nationally recognized speaker in the financial services industry, hosts a weekly webinar show called Free Webinar Wednesdays and is a graduate from the Graduate School of Banking at the University of Wisconsin in Madison, WI, in 2003. He now serves on GSB's faculty teaching on the topics of social technology. Cook earned his MBA in 1999 and holds undergraduate degrees in business administration and psychology.

He helps his clients in the areas of web development, search marketing and optimization, social media strategies, e-mail marketing and "big-picture" digital strategic planning. Cook is a member of the National Speakers Association as well as a certified auditor with Socially Legal Audit™. When he's not helping his clients succeed on the Internet, he can typically be found on one of his many bicycles training for his next triathlon or mountain bike race.

Miko Kershberg

 Miko Kershberg is an Internet marketing expert located in Antwerp, Belgium. Miko has been an Internet Marketing Consultant with WSI for the last 4 years and the representative for Europe on the WSI Internet Consultants Advisory Council.

Certified for web and Google analytics, as well as conversion optimization, Miko is passionate about laying the proper foundations, using search to drive traffic, measuring results and improving the digital marketing efforts of and for his clients.